WHAT'S IN YOUR BACKPACK?

Copyright© 2024 Rohini Rathour

Published by Known Publishing, 2024

The right of Rohini Rathour to be identified
as the Author of the Work has been asserted by her in
accordance with the Copyright, Designs and Patents Act 1988.
All rights reserved.

Illustrations by Yuvi Rathour

Paperback: 978-1-915850-26-3

Ebook: 978-1-915850-27-0

This book is sold subject to the condition it shall not, by way of trade
or otherwise, be circulated in any form or by any means, electronic or
otherwise, without the publisher's prior consent.

WWW.GET-KNOWN.CO.UK

For Priya

Go free, my darling Priya
Fly like a seagull
Float like a feather
Smile through a flower
Shine like the star you are
Glow as the flame of a candle
Talk to me through a song
Touch me with your laugh
Warm me with your presence
It will take time
To adjust to this new you
Until we meet again

FOREWORD

Navigating the path of personal growth can be challenging, and having a trusted guide can make all the difference. *What's In Your Backpack?* serves as that trusted guide, masterfully bridging the gap between practical guidance and timeless wisdom. In a world that often feels overwhelming and chaotic, this work stands as a beacon of clarity and inspiration, guiding us to a deeper understanding of ourselves and our journey through life.

From the very first page, I realised that this book is not merely a collection of ideas but a transformative journey. It invites us to explore the metaphor of the invisible backpack - a concept so skillfully utilised by Rohini Rathour - that deeply resonates with my own experiences. This metaphor perfectly encapsulates how our life experiences, belief systems, and emotional baggage shape who we are. And Rohini's adept use of the metaphor helps us recognise the weight we carry and provides invaluable insights into how this weight influences our lives.

Drawing inspiration from Dr. Joe Dispenza's notion that, by age 35, much of who we are becomes automatic, *What's In Your Backpack* invites us to re-examine our autopilot setting. It encourages us to become conscious of the contents of our backpack, and provides practical tools to reshape and redefine them. In my own life, this kind of introspection has been a catalyst for meaningful change, and I can attest to the power of addressing and transforming our deep-seated patterns.

We carry far more in our backpack than we realise, and it impacts us each and every day.

At the heart of this book is the concept of abundance - not as a material goal but as a mindset that opens us to the limitless resources available in our lives. Rohini's exploration of abundance aligns with my own experience of recognising the limitless resources available to us and embracing trust in the universe's ability to meet our needs. With this mindset, you will learn to ask clearly for what you need and to trust that life will respond in its own way. And as straightforward as that may sound, it's no small thing to actualise.

In addition to its exploration of abundance, *What's In Your Backpack* introduces the 7C's framework, which I find to be a highly practical guide designed to help you navigate both the inner and outer aspects of your life. Each of these 7C's is illuminated with thoughtful exercises, stories, and reflective prompts, making it easier for you to integrate these principles into your daily life. This framework is not only insightful but highly actionable, echoing the valuable transformative practices that have guided my own journey of growth and fulfilment.

As you begin this book, I encourage you to approach it with an open mind and a willingness to think about yourself and life in ways you may not have before. Let Rohini's insights and stories inspire you as you continue on your own path of self-discovery. May this journey offer you new perspectives and a deeper understanding of yourself.

With light,

Leon VanderPol

Founder & CEO, Center for Transformational Coaching. Author of *A Shift in Being: The Art and Practices of Deep Transformational Coaching*

CONTENTS

INTRODUCTION	**11**
PART 1	**15**
The backpack and its impact on your health and personality	16
Proactively restore balance and inner harmony in your body	19
Time to look inside that backpack	22
This book is a doorway to self-discovery	26
What having me as your coach would look like	28
How this book will help you	30
Awareness, Acknowledgment and Acceptance	33
Being Me	37
PART 2	**41**
Contextualising the problem	42
A quest to thrive, not just survive	44
You are unique, but not alone	48
How this problem comes about	49
Why I wrote this book	52
Become the creator of your future	55
Why we become prisoners of status quo	58
Turning unconscious reactions into conscious responses	67
PART 3	**69**
Why we don't always know what we really want	70
Your inner world and your outer world	74

The first step is self-awareness	75
The role of upbringing in the development of personality	77
Becoming a monk – silence, space and stillness	82
Life is a stage – the role others play	85
Knowing what you want and asking for it	87
Unconditional Love	94
PART 4	**97**
Bringing you the 7C's	99
1. Curiosity	101
2. Creativity	113
3. Competence	127
4. Connection	144
5. Communication	166
6. Conflict	181
7. Clarity	202
PART 5	**225**
No such thing as an ordinary life	226
My journey to becoming the coach my younger self needed	227
Create your abundant life	230
Creating a strong financial foundation	244
Discernment of value	245
Conclusion	247
ACKNOWLEDGEMENTS	**254**
ABOUT THE AUTHOR	**256**

INTRODUCTION

"95% of who you are, by the time you're 35 years old, is a set of memorised behaviours, skills, emotional reactions, beliefs, perceptions and attitudes that functions like an automatic computer programme. So, 95% of who you are is a subconscious or even an unconscious state of being."

DR JOE DISPENZA, YOU ARE THE PLACEBO.

This book is about abundance, backpacks and the 7C's. Let me introduce you to my understanding of each of these in turn.

Abundance

Abundance is about access, not ownership. It is knowing that everything you will ever need is either within you or is accessible to you from an external source. Abundance is knowing that when you have a need for something, your need will be met.

Abundance is about getting clear on what you want and learning how to ask for it. The universe loves a clear request, to which there is one of three possible answers: *yes*, *not yet*, or *something better awaits you*. It is about trust that what is meant for you will always be with you when the time is right.

Abundance is about faith and a willingness to go with the flow. Not forcibly or passively, but by being present to life knowing that we don't always know what lies ahead, and that it is not necessary to be in control every step of the way.

Abundance is about being resourceful, even when you don't have all the resources. It is believing that you are more ready than you think you are.

Abundance begins with a vision of what is possible and having the courage to step out into the unknown without knowing what lies ahead.

The backpack

When you were born, imagine you came into this world with an invisible backpack. From the moment you became aware of your surroundings, your backpack began to have things added to it. As you heard voices, saw faces, felt the touch of familiar and less familiar hands, experienced sensations of hunger, satiation, joy, isolation, safety, and so much more, your body tucked every one of these experiences into this backpack.

For illustrative purposes only, let's assume that in the first year of your life, before you could take your first steps or communicate with language, you were like a sponge in one-way absorption mode. By the time you were a year old, your backpack had a kilo's weight in the form of accumulated learning, experiences and emotions.

Thereon, your net growth rate in your backpack is about 1% per month. This means that whatever you already have in your backpack is augmented with a further 1% of such "stuff" as a result of living and interacting with the external world. By the time you are 25 years old, your backpack weighs over 17 kilos. By the time you get to 40, you are carrying around 105 kilos of a lifetime's accumulation of baggage!

This is the power of compounding. It assumes that every new experience or stimulus is absorbed and assimilated into your being, building on a rapidly growing base. What you already have inside this backpack is also growing and morphing with time. If we could have such growth in our savings and investments, this would be a deeply desirable outcome that would result in exponential returns. However, when it comes to our emotions and behaviours, particularly the negative ones, this kind of seemingly uncontrolled growth is detrimental to our physical, emotional and mental wellbeing. It is the root cause of many physical illnesses, including chronic and life-limiting diseases.

The 7C's framework

This is a simple framework with which to navigate our inner world and the outer world. The twists and turns, the ups and downs of everyday life can feel like being on a small boat sailing across the seven seas of being human. Each C is already a part of what you do, how you live and why you love or loathe your life. A significant part of this book is devoted to exploring and elaborating on each C, with a list of exercises at the end of each chapter to help you become more mindful of how you perceive them when they show up in your life and what actions you choose to take.

I expect you will get to the end of each chapter, shake your head and say "I already knew that!" You might wonder why something so obvious needed to be written about. That will be a good outcome. You already know everything there is to know, but sometimes it takes a prompt to remind you how to turn that knowing into a life experience. I hope my book will be that prompt for you. I hope it will help you steer your little boat of human existence with greater purpose and confidence, and get to the shores of your abundant life.

In Part 1 we will explore why this metaphorical backpack is key to our health and our ability to navigate our way through this world. I will also explain what this book aims to do and how it can help you. In Part 2 I offer examples of the kinds of problems we sometimes face but can't explain why we feel that way. I offer a few examples of what people might call first-world problems that can be painful nevertheless. In Part 3 we will look at potential ways to overcome these problems using the inside out approach and lay the groundwork for the 7C's framework. In Part 4 we cover each of the 7C's in some detail with exercises to help you understand and internalise its meaning in your own life. In Part 5 we bring it all together offering you a practical framework for creating your very own abundant life.

PART 1

PART 1

THE BACKPACK AND ITS IMPACT ON YOUR HEALTH AND PERSONALITY

By the time you get to 35, your invisible backpack is already quite heavy. In line with the growth indicated by my earlier calculations, it weighs 58 kilos. You're still accumulating stuff on autopilot and there is less energy for discernment in terms of what kind of stuff you are adding to your bulging backpack.

The mid-thirties in most people's lives tend to be dominated by commitment and responsibilities. They're likely to be in a career that demands much of their time and energy whilst also having families to provide and care for. There may be little time for pausing, reflecting and letting go.

You might yearn for new experiences. You might long for an ecosystem that rejuvenates your body and relaxes the spirit. But all the above reasons stop you from getting there. After all, there are only so many hours in the day and no one has infinite reserves of energy. The path of least resistance feels easier. Old habits and thought patterns run effortlessly on well worn grooves.

The old and familiar ground is a better option when you're carrying a heavy load and every step feels laboured. It doesn't feel like the right time to explore an exciting new terrain that may be full of ups and downs, littered with uncertain twists and turns. Can you now see how living on autopilot can translate into becoming ever more set in our ways with a personality that seems hard to change?

I once had a client in his late thirties who found it difficult to communicate with his business partners. He disagreed with them on important strategic and operational aspects of the business, but he could not articulate an alternative that he would be happier with. His was a path of least resistance and passive aggression in the face of what he saw as unreasonable demands. His stonewalling, uncommunicative behaviour was causing a great deal of friction in the boardroom.

The problem was that he believed his personality was now set for life. He saw no point in others wishing for him to change his ways. He would have preferred it if they simply accepted him for who and what he was and learned to work around it. The impasse and the resulting conflict was detracting from the exciting possibilities that lay ahead for the business.

People with my client's mindset will typically go along to get along. They avoid conflict, and when faced with it, don't deal with it well. This includes becoming stubborn, pretending to agree but not really following up with the right actions and avoiding communication altogether. They might fear that in the process of communicating, they may inadvertently upset the other person and create more dreaded conflict. This in turn leads to a detachment and disconnection with anything and anyone who might upset the status quo.

People in such a position might be holding in a lot of frustration, angst and resentment – like a dormant volcano. If prodded or provoked excessively, they can erupt in ways that are shocking to those who've never known them to behave like that. In some cases, the eruption happens within the body in the form of a serious physical or mental illness that forces the person to finally stop, take notice and make a change.

PART 1

In my client's case, coaching was a safe space in which he saw himself as others saw him. It also helped him see what his behaviour was doing to him. He saw how his actions were affecting the most important people in his life. He also came to understand what lay beneath their behaviour towards him. This was the first step towards greater self-awareness. Such an expansion of perspective to include what others might be experiencing when interacting with you is a powerful catalyst for change. In his case, a change of perspective led to a willingness to change his mindset.

He realised that his old mindset meant that he was going through the motions doing things that no longer gave him the joy they once did. He recognised that he had lost his drive, even though he viewed himself as an ambitious person. His ambitions now felt like a pipe dream. He had no energy to pursue them and increasingly told himself he had to learn to live with what he had rather than rock the boat in search of something new.

In that state, my client was entrenched in a state of functional apathy: an illusion of being busy but feeling stuck in a lesser life. The first step was to get clear on what he really wanted and then take the necessary actions towards them. This included having an honest conversation with his business partners, holding firm on what was important to him and finding a middle ground to work from.

When those discussions were had with openness and without judgement, they realised that they all wanted the same outcome even if they disagreed on how to get there. This was a huge step in the right direction which opened up the field for exploring possibilities and choosing one that they all agreed with.

That takes courage. The courage to let go of a way of life that has become a habit. The courage to disappoint people who have become accustomed to the old you. The courage to embrace a new life that is unknown and uncertain. The courage to try something different knowing you might fail.

As a coach, I am the client's companion and guide on a small part of their journey. The 7C's is a framework I created back in 2017, and one I use as a guide to help clients navigate their way through uncertainty and change. The journey begins with finding the courage to set down your heavy backpack and take a peek inside with compassion and love for yourself.

PROACTIVELY RESTORE BALANCE AND INNER HARMONY IN YOUR BODY

The subconscious mind is like a supercomputer that is the repository of all the information that exists in the universe. The human body is the device that helps connect with this supercomputer.

Think about your phone. It is the portal to a whole wide world of information that is now at your fingertips. As you add more and more programs, apps and information, you use up the limited storage on your phone.

What happens if you let this accumulation continue unabated? How often do you have to delete stuff that's taking up storage? Or update your phone with better software or a new battery? Or simply replace it with a new one?

Like the phone, our human body can also get clogged up and slows down when it becomes overloaded. When we release trapped emotions, we are freeing up the body of energies that keep it stuck in unhelpful patterns. We create space for new, more positive experiences that help us move forward feeling lighter and more energised.

Our body is far more intelligent and resilient than we can conceive in our wildest imagination. Think about all the things we do every second of our life without knowing it or controlling it. It's only when we lose one of our faculties that we realise how much we took for granted and how foolish we were to not take better care of our body.

Aside from being utterly amazing, our body is also incredibly forgiving. It has the power to heal and restore itself. Birth and death are no strangers to our bodies with cells dying and being reborn every second of our life.

An article in the *Scientific American* issue of 1st April 2021 explores the human body's ability to replace billions of cells every day, with blood and gut dominating cell turnover. The tiny cells in our bloodstream live between 3 and 120 days. In fact, the cells that form the lining of our gut have a typical lifespan of less than a week.

"Those two groups therefore make up the giant majority of the turnover. About 330 billion cells are replaced daily, equivalent to about one percent of all our cells. In 80 to 100 days, 30 trillion will have replenished – the equivalent of a new you", the article goes on to say.

These intelligent cells are not only seamlessly communicating with one another to ensure the smooth functioning of our body, but they are also communicating with our consciousness in a wordless language. If we paid more attention, we might understand what it is trying to say, and do what is needed to restore inner balance and harmony.

Our society prioritises external communication in languages that are expressed through writing and speaking. The secret and silent language of the body is often missed or drowned out. We only become aware that something is wrong within us when we feel discomfort, pain or unease. These are equivalent to the body shouting out loud because we were not listening to its quiet warnings.

Canadian physician and author Dr Gabor Maté has been one of the leading voices on the cost of stress and trapped emotions on our bodies. In his book *When The Body Says No - The Cost of Hidden Stress*, Dr Maté offers insights and examples of how the body keeps track and remembers everything, even if we don't consciously recall most of our experiences.

Despite the fact that our physical body is constantly changing from within, the cellular memory does not die with the physical cells. These memories of past traumas and positive experiences live within us in the form of energy. Energy can neither be created nor destroyed, but it can be transferred or transformed. It can move within our body or be expelled outwards in positive or negative ways, and we have some choice and control over this process.

Notice what's going on with you, inside you. You're feeling uncharacteristically tired? You're losing your temper at events and people who don't deserve your ire? Your lower back hurts and your migraines are back? The doctors are unable to find anything medically that explains these symptoms. You feel fed up and helpless. It could be a result of trapped emotions that you are not conscious of.

Dr Bradley Nelson's book *The Emotion Code* provides further examples of how trapped emotions cause unexplained physical and mental imbalances. He has also created a non-intrusive, painless and simple way with which to identify and release trapped emotions with tens of thousands of testimonials on its benefits. My clients and I have had first hand experience of this and also benefited from it.

Becoming more conscious of the secret language of your body is the first step to making meaningful choices and taking the right action. It is the most important step towards healing and restoring balance in your life.

TIME TO LOOK INSIDE THAT BACKPACK

By the time we are in our thirties, our personality is largely a function of the habits we've learnt over our lifetimes. Our body becomes our mind, having stored memories of our past experiences, mixed with thought and emotion. Before too long, our life has become a series of routines with little room for change or inspiration. We may be unaware of the things we do or why we do them. It is only when we see ourselves as others see us that we become conscious of these patterns of behaviour.

It's time to slow down, take a pause to put down your backpack and look inside. It will be daunting. Not unlike decluttering the home where you've lived your entire life. A place that houses memories and emotions you've accumulated over your lifetime, making you who you are. This home is none other than your body. The one you were born in. The home of your spirit while you are on this earth.

Observe the contents of your bulging, back-breakingly heavy backpack. Amongst all the clutter and seemingly useless stuff there are valuable lessons, gifts and limitations that make you the unique individual you are. There are maps, tools and guides you've always had helping you navigate your way through the human experience called life.

First, there's the external backpack. It starts filling up when you become aware of the external world, the ecosystem you've lived in, the norms and expectations of the family you've grown up with. With time and practice, you become more accomplished and confident at dealing with these external stimuli. You may even enjoy the challenge and thrive in the glow of external validation gained from a job well done. Achievement becomes a measure of success and personal identity. Before long, your self-worth has become tied with external validation. You are viewed as reliable, dependable, conscientious, diligent, responsible, loyal, and so on. The more willing you are to carry the load of a new challenge, a more onerous responsibility, the more load is added to your backpack.

One of the most commonly felt negative emotions amongst successful people is guilt. Guilt that you're not doing enough. Guilt that your success means someone else's failure. Guilt that despite having it all you still want more, and what that says about you. Guilt is often the darker side of gratitude. You might feel that you have so much to be grateful for. And yet deep down you want something else.

PART 1

You want more. You feel guilty for wanting more when you know you are so much better off than many out there. You feel guilty that wanting a different life makes you selfish, especially if it is not what others in your life want.

This book will help you to slow down and notice what you're carrying in this external backpack. It will help you discover why you chose to take on that load. And most importantly, it will help you decide whether that burden is yours to carry, and if yes, in what shape and form.

Next, there's the internal baggage in the form of sensations, memories and emotions. Every stimulus triggers a feeling that in turn spawns thousands of thoughts. Our thoughts and feelings feed off one another, sparking sensations and bodily responses that we might not be consciously aware of. Put them together and we have a myriad of emotions that are driving our behaviour.

An emotion becomes trapped when we either suppress it, repress it, inadequately or counterproductively express it. Not all trapped emotions are negative. But the fact that they are trapped suggests avoidance, resistance and an absence of flow.

Let's take an example of a person who has never experienced a loving relationship having grown up in a family where love was absent. As an adult, they may not know how to recognise feelings of love or be romantic with their significant other. They might come across as emotionally unavailable and lose the opportunity to be in an intimate and loving relationship.

In another instance, a person may have grown up being told it was unbecoming to laugh out loud or appear too happy. As an adult they might find it difficult to be spontaneous or do things just for fun.

Or let's say you were told that talking openly about your wins is tantamount to ugly boasting. Now you're an adult working in a competitive field, you find it difficult to confidently advocate for yourself or command credit for the work you've done.

Every time we experience an event that triggers feelings that are hard to process, creating thoughts that are uncomfortable, we add them to our hoard of unprocessed emotions. Emotion is, after all, energy in motion. Over time, like dormant volcanoes, these internal wells of trapped energy begin to get restless and turn toxic. They make their unseen presence known in many different ways, most of which are unhealthy.

These trapped energies navigate their way around the body and may take residence in places where we can't help but notice them. They might call out to us in the form of physical pain or discomfort. We may experience medically unexplained migraines, stiffness in the back of the neck and shoulders, joint pain, arthritis, asthma, a frozen shoulder, lower back pain and so on. Or they might make their presence known through unexplained bouts of panic, anxiety, anger or sadness. And in some cases, these unprocessed emotions of a lifetime can manifest into chronic, debilitating and even life-limiting illnesses.

The contents of our external backpack are often the very same things that create the bubbling lava of unseen trapped emotions within.

Too much responsibility can result in frustration and resentment. *Why do I have to do everything? Why can't people do things properly like I do?*

Obligations can result in feelings of anxiety, guilt and shame. *I have a lifestyle and status to maintain which means I have to keep doing what I'm doing, even if I long to do something else. I have so much to be grateful for, I feel guilty for wanting a different life.*

Commitments can bring feelings of fear, rejection, disappointment and sadness. *I have put so much of myself into this relationship, I can't let it fail or let go. What if they leave me? What if I no longer belong here?*

Come with me on a journey of self-discovery. Observe, notice and acknowledge what you find. Appreciate the gifts and treasures. Let go of things that are past their use-by date. Now is the time to make space for the new, allowing light into the dark unexplored depths of your very being. Lighten your load. Flow and fly more freely through life.

THIS BOOK IS A DOORWAY TO SELF-DISCOVERY

First and foremost, I hope you will enjoy reading this book. It is a labour of love. I am a visual and experiential learner. I love using analogies, metaphors and stories. They are intended to bring the concepts of this book to life and make them more relatable.

I am also easily distracted and often veer off down a new rabbit hole of curiosity. You might sometimes feel like I've taken you by the hand on an Alice in Wonderland kind of adventure. I want you to feel as if it is just you and me, and that we are having a conversation, albeit a very one-sided one.

I am going to be very presumptuous in believing that you will read this book more than once. On your first reading you might choose to skim the book from start to finish and get a sense of what it's all about before returning to it more intentionally.

Or you might be the kind of person who is unhurried from the start and takes their time to really absorb each section at leisure, and faithfully work through the reflections and exercises as you come upon them.

Each chapter on the 7C's ends in a section with some suggested exercises. They are there to help you reflect on what you've read and process it before you move on. You only truly learn when you put what you know into practice.

However you choose to read it, I want you to know that I am energetically with you as your compassionate guide. The concepts and stories might spark something in you – a recognition, a knowing, or just pure divine inspiration. Write them all down. Those a-ha moments are powerful and you might not remember them later.

You might even find it is more useful to work with a partner or friend or a book club. Discussions can further bring concepts to life and deepen understanding from multiple perspectives. Working with a partner or buddy is a fun and less solitary way to unpack and unburden yourself. It will help you see yourself through someone else's eyes.

Finding a person who will hold a mirror up to us in a supportive and non-judgemental way is how we become more self-aware and make changes on a conscious basis. If you can't find such a person in your personal or professional network, find yourself a coach. A coach will help you get from where you are to where you want to be faster than if you go it alone.

Unlike a well-intentioned friend or family member, a coach has the advantage of having no preconceptions or judgements about you; they can be objective whilst being compassionate. Coaching is not therapy, but coaching can be therapeutic. Having a safe and supportive space in which to explore what's happening in your life can create big shifts from within and be life-changing.

According to a 2009 International Coaching Federation Global Coaching Study, 95% of people who hire coaches rated them "good" or "excellent". 68% of the individuals who hired coaches made their investment back. Coaching is an intangible service and the benefits to clients are often priceless. Those who do make a financial gain as a result of coaching were found on average to have made 3.4x the money they spent. In other words, if they invested £10,000 on coaching, they made £34,000 back. The top 20% made a return of 50x.

Despite these compelling statistics, the majority of the population considers coaching to be remedial or a luxury. In the workplace, being told you "should work with a coach" is often met with dismay: *"What's wrong with me? Why do I need a coach?"*

WHAT HAVING ME AS YOUR COACH WOULD LOOK LIKE

This book offers you a taste of what working with me might look and feel like. There is no template or process to achieving your desired outcome. Instead, I present you with a toolbox, a set of principles and philosophies that have worked for me and the people I have coached. I draw on my own experiences and the wisdom of a diverse range of experts who have helped me along the way. You are the best judge of what is right for you.

If you've experienced deep trauma and are living with the consequences of it, this book may present food for thought, but some of its exercises may prove triggering and might cause you to relive old hurts. Please listen to your body and do what feels right for you. This book is not a substitute for working with a qualified counsellor or therapist.

Coaching works when the person being coached really wants to be coached and is willing to fully engage and commit to turning insights into action. They must be willing to come in with an open mind, to face some uncomfortable truths and take necessary action to replace old unconscious habits with new conscious ones.

Every one of us is unique. After a lifetime of conformity, it is an eye-opener to discover your uniqueness and how you are making a difference in this world. When you have someone who believes in you, your world changes. When you believe in yourself, you can change the world.

As your coach, I begin with the premise that you already have all that you need to know, even if you are not aware of it. The greatest living expert on you is you. However, even experts have blind spots. You may be too close to yourself to see yourself as others see you. You may be too focused on the things about yourself that need improving or changing, and not enough on your gifts and strengths.

Furthermore, you might be focusing on areas of your personality that you are consciously aware of. And as we've said before, that could at best be 5% of who you really are. Giving yourself space, time and energy to observe what's really going on beneath the surface and seeking answers from within will transform your life.

PART 1

HOW THIS BOOK WILL HELP YOU

This book is for you if you're simply curious and open minded. Perhaps you're a fan of personal development and enjoy reading self-help books. I warmly welcome you. This book is written as an easy read, with liberal use of analogies, metaphors, anecdotes and real-life stories to bring concepts to life.

Perhaps you are looking for a book that will inspire you to be more present to life and feel more in balance. Something is missing. You might not be depressed or sad. But you're lacking the spontaneous, joyful energy you once effortlessly exuded. You want to create a fuller, happier, more meaningful life but don't know what that looks like or how to create it. You want to play to your strengths, use the gifts and tools that lie idly within you. You are motivated by what's possible for you but feel trapped in your current reality.

Or perhaps you feel weighed down by the responsibilities of your everyday life that you willingly shoulder. You're experiencing unexplained bouts of guilt, anger, dissatisfaction, frustration, anxiety or even sadness. These negative emotions sap your energy and life force. They taint your relationships and put a dampener on everything that should be good in your life. On the surface, all seems good. To outsiders your life may even seem perfect. But you feel stuck. You want something else, but you don't know what that is or how you will get there.

You may be reading this book because you sense a disconnect between how you see yourself and how the world sees you. You feel like an imposter, a fraud. Your life hasn't turned out how you imagined it would. There's simmering discontent deep within you, like a dormant volcano that could erupt with no warning. You want to understand what is weighing you down from within, holding you back. You long for harmony and balance between your inner world of thoughts and feelings, and the outer world you physically inhabit.

This book will help you get to know yourself better. You will see yourself more clearly, through a more curious and compassionate lens. You will understand why you do the things you do and what else is possible for you. You will see that not all choices are mutually exclusive: you can replace "or" with "and" and create an abundant life.

This sounds simple, but we know it is far from easy. There are an infinite number of possibilities and variables. We have no control on the workings of the outer world, but we can connect and control what's going on inside us. We can look inside the backpack. It can feel a little daunting, even scary. What if we find something we don't like? What if there are things in there that we can't change or let go of?

It's the what ifs that can be the greatest barrier. They breed doubt and fear within us. They remind us that we are not in control, that there are dangers lurking in that vast unknown.

How about we replace *what if* with *what is* and trust that you chose this life with all its manifold twists and turns? How would it feel to let go of any illusion of control and surrender to the flow of life?

Before you can flow, you must let go. If you want to fly, you need to travel light. This book will offer you reasons to pause and reflect. To take time each day to stop for a while, put down your backpack and look inside. You may find in there things you'd long forgotten about, or had actively suppressed. You will learn to become aware of them, acknowledge their existence with courage and accept them with compassion.

This book is your guide on a journey of gentle self-inquiry and awareness. My insights are mixed with the stories and experiences of people who are on a similar journey. They shared their stories with me: the qualities that helped them get to where they are, who their key influences were, the negative emotions they most frequently experienced and how they dealt with adversity and the unknown. Some of these individuals have worked with me. Others have followed my work and enthusiastically agreed to be part of this book.

In their stories you may see your own situation and dilemmas reflected back, helping you to feel less alone. The simple exercises in this book invite you to take action and put what you learn into practice. It is only through conscious action that real change can happen. This book will give you the tools to experience your inner world in a more compassionate way, let go of the things that no longer serve you and create space for new opportunities, people and experiences.

Are you ready for a radically different life that you only ever fantasised about? Are you ready to get to the bottom of what you are actually afraid of? Are you ready to make possibility, not pain, your catalyst for change?

AWARENESS, ACKNOWLEDGMENT AND ACCEPTANCE

It is impossible to feel light and liberated without addressing what is causing you to feel so weighed down. In a three-step process of awareness, acknowledgment and acceptance, we can come to terms with what's happening, why it is happening and choose what to do with that knowledge. Understanding why we feel the way we do helps us become more accepting of ourselves. It is only when you truly accept yourself for who you are that you can evolve into the person you are meant to be.

Over the coming chapters, I will offer you tools that help you see yourself in a more compassionate and non-judgemental light. Most of our unconscious habits are a result of strategies we deployed as children and young adults. Strategies that enabled us to cope with a challenging world, to interact better with the people in our lives who were in a position of power or influence. These strategies have usually kept us safe, sane and alive. We may have forgotten why we chose these particular ways of behaving, and now we do them on autopilot, even in situations where a different approach might be needed.

Awareness is the first step to making any change. Once you acknowledge, understand and accept what's going on inside of you, you are then in a better place to choose your next steps. One of those initial steps might be to work with a coach, a therapist or a counsellor.

Most of my life I believed that staying self-sufficient, resilient and optimistic is the best way to be. Like many others, I was conditioned by the fact that most people prefer not to be around those who express negative emotions, such as anger, fear and sadness. Avoiding conflict and keeping the peace became the mantra of my life.

Having been through a few significant challenges in my own life, I began to notice how I processed (or didn't process) my negative emotions. I had become very good at "forgetting" unpleasant events and moving on as quickly as possible. It helped me to not dwell on things that would only make me upset. Every so often, these suppressed emotions would rise up causing me to feel overwhelmed. Occasionally, I would react with outrage mixed with tears that would become a source of embarrassment for me and those who witnessed it. I would apologise for my overreaction and resolved to get better at suppressing those unpleasant emotions.

A few years ago, after I'd left my corporate job and was looking for ways to deal with the challenges in my own life, I read Dr Gabor Maté's *When The Body Says No: The Cost of Hidden Stress*. Dr Maté is a Canadian-Hungarian physician who has over the decades worked in general practice, in addiction clinics and in palliative care units. It was a compelling account of the toll suppressed negative emotions take on our bodies. It made me see how mistaken I had been to not deal with my negative emotions in a healthy way and how I was storing up trouble that might impact me later in life.

A bit like colours, emotions come in a vast spectrum with so many different shades. Like most people, I was aware of the basic emotions – sad, happy, angry, scared, disappointed and so on. I now realise that clustered around each core emotion are many subtler emotions that have names and frequencies that are uniquely theirs. This influences how that particular emotion manifests in our body, how we might express it (knowingly or not) and what we can do to deal with it in a healthy way.

For instance, adjacent to the core emotion of anger sit emotions of frustration, resentment, petulance, stubbornness, bitterness, hatred and feeling peeved and so on. A person who goes through life feeling perpetually frustrated and resentful might be completely unaware that they are angry. I'm not an angry person, they might protest. They may have never shouted at anyone or been physically threatening or violent. But the anger is undoubtedly being expressed or held in ways that are unhealthy. Become aware of the emotion, acknowledge it by name and accept its presence. Sitting with the emotion and going within to understand its trigger can help connect the dots and identify the root cause. Once we've taken these steps, we are ready to let it go.

You can do this by taking a few minutes each day to check in with yourself. If an event or interaction triggered a negative feeling in you that you could not express or process at the time, make sure to sit with that feeling when you have a quiet few minutes. Imagine that your attention holds that feeling by the hand and on the carriage of your breath does an inward scan of your body. Allow the emotion to point you to the areas in the body where it hides when you're too busy to pay attention. They might be where you experience some pain, or tightness or heaviness.

Simply noticing each emotion and its resting place without trying to intervene is in itself very therapeutic. Accept

PART 2

its presence with compassion for yourself; for the fallible, imperfect human that you are. Self-compassion is not selfish. You will get better at spotting the emotion the next time it is generated within you. You will learn to make better, more self-honouring choices and to treat yourself with the same kindness you would treat others. That is the way to live a balanced, healthy and fulfilled life. I am on a quest to create such a life for myself, and with all my heart, I wish the same for you.

BEING ME

I'm not a poet
The words come to me
When I open my heart
And set myself free.

How does it feel
When I look at me?
All I see is
A flawed human being.

Until I connect with
The child who was me
Spontaneous and joyful
As perfect as can be.

Tired of being looked at
Craving to be seen
To meet that one person
Who gets where I've been.

I ask myself the question
Why do I overshare?
Is it in the hope that
Someone will care?

Be vulnerable, they say
Share all your pain
But be careful, I think
It might all be in vain.

Pain and struggles abound
Challenges galore
But I'll stick with my own
Not swap them for yours.

People will judge
Based on what they see
Not knowing it's a mask
That hides the real me.

The mask is no lie
It's who I want to be
In the future I'm creating
That person is me.

How will I get
From here to there?
The journey is long
With no time to spare.

Will I have company
Or go on my own?
Fear not, a voice tells me
You're never alone.

Everything I'll ever need
Is inside of me
First I must go deep within
And learn how to be.

There's a vast Universe
That is my friend
Love, acceptance and belief
Are vital in the end.

You are unique and amazing
With so much to give
Learning to love yourself
Will change how you live.

My story is yours
And I see yours in mine
This poem is both personal
And universal at the same time.

PART 2

PART 2

CONTEXTUALISING THE PROBLEM

Imagine that your life is like a house with five or more rooms. There is a room each for your work, your close family, your friends and extended family, for you to spend "me-time" doing what matters to you, and finally a room for the community projects and activities that may have no direct connection to any of the other rooms.

When your life is in balance and you are feeling in harmony, you spend quality time in every one of these rooms. You are fully present in whatever room you enter and the room receives your undivided attention. Even if you don't spend the same amount of time in each room, the time you do spend is intentional, with your mind, heart and senses all present. You radiate positive energy. You create, attract and thrive in abundance.

The reality of our daily life is that, in this metaphorical house, we spend disproportionate amounts of time in one or two rooms. Even when we are in one of the other rooms, we're not all there. For instance, we may be with our family at the dinner table, but we're still thinking about that difficult meeting we had with our boss, worrying about what that means for our promotion prospects. In another instance, we're in a work meeting but our thoughts keep returning to the argument we had with our partner just before leaving home. In both examples, we are physically present but our mind is elsewhere.

This has a direct impact on the flow of our energy. Your energy flows to the place where your attention goes. When you are not truly present, the people you are with and the tasks you've been entrusted with are getting short-changed. You are going through the motions hoping no one will notice. But people do notice. We just know when someone's not really with us. This is detrimental to your relationship and to your levels of productivity.

The body has three centres of intelligence: the heart, the mind and the gut. In our noisy, fractious and stressful world, it is rare that individuals go through life with their three centres of intelligence all in agreement and balance. Most of the time your head is telling you to do something that your heart doesn't agree with, and the gut is keeping quiet because you've stopped listening to it. It's no wonder that so many of us go through life feeling out of kilter.

For the purpose of this book, I decided to speak to individuals who were willing to share their experiences of self-discovery and personal development with me. Some are clients who've worked with me over varying periods of time. These individuals are all highly educated professionals and are aged between the late-twenties and mid-fifties. Their qualifications might set them apart as amongst the highly educated professional elite, but most of these individuals had humble beginnings. They've worked hard, and in some cases had to overcome prejudice to get to where they are. Some grew up in small provincial towns, brought up in communities that lacked facilities and opportunities those in the larger cities take for granted. A few were the first in their family to go to university.

As a result of the natural process of self-selection, all my interviewees are more self-aware than the average person. Some started young, journaling, reading about self-help and spirituality, and talking openly about feelings. Family dynamics and role models influenced their view of the world. Some became introspective as life threw curveballs at them in the form of heartbreak, illness or some other kind of loss. A few suffered the tragedy of losing a parent that cruelly interrupted their childhood and resulted in them having to grow up too soon.

I've used their first names or pseudonyms to protect their privacy. Their stories and experiences are personal to them, but the insights are universal. I sprinkle these over the coming chapters, like fairy dust, to bring the concepts in this book vividly to life.

A QUEST TO THRIVE, NOT JUST SURVIVE

You might be one of the success stories with a great job, a dream home, and a beautiful family. On paper your life is perfect. And yet, inside there is an emptiness that all the professional accolades and money in the bank cannot fill. There is an absence of joy and a desire for something else that you can't quite put a finger on. You feel lost and unfulfilled despite the illusion of going places and having everything. Below are examples of people whose inner turmoil was stopping them from living their best life.

Tara – a business executive and new mum

Tara is a woman in her early thirties with a young baby. She's a graduate of a top business school and is working at a well-known e-commerce corporate giant. Before she had her baby, she was ambitious and had clear career goals. When she returned from maternity leave, she noticed things had changed in her workplace. She was placed in a different team with a new manager who wasn't really familiar with her previous work or what she was capable of. Where previously she'd have willingly worked 14-hour days and sacrificed weekends, she now resented the fact that it took her away from her baby. The job she had once enjoyed was now dominated by menial tasks that someone more junior could have done. She no longer knew where her career with this particular company was going. She felt like she was being set up for failure by a manager who didn't care what happened to her.

In our coaching sessions, she confessed that she would love to quit and spend more time with her baby, but she feared that doing so would lower her standing in the eyes of her family and her peer group. She was also anxious about losing her financial independence and being treated as a person of little worth. Consequently, she'd stayed in her job despite the heaviness and the stuckness of her working life.

Tara needed to see that she had a choice; that there is always another way forward. The chains that held her imprisoned in her unhappy working life were held together by her own fears and feelings of insecurity. It would take courage to explore an alternative way of life.

Sam – a business consultant wanting to avoid burnout

Sam is a business consultant who quit his job after six successful but gruelling years. He feared he would burn out if he carried on and he was keen to explore something different, perhaps work for a start-up, with a view to one day starting his own company. This was a bold move. Most people in his circle ensured they had a job to go to before resigning.

With every passing week that he was "unemployed" he felt the growing burden of scrutiny and the weight of expectations. He had a notion of what the "right next move" was for him, and he was convinced that anything less would result in him being judged by his peer group. He feared he'd disappoint his close circle of family and friends who had high hopes for him. This made him doubt himself and feel anxious about his future.

In our coaching sessions, he'd tell me going on LinkedIn was torture because it reminded him that he was at a standstill while everyone else out there seemed to be powering ahead. In his moments of self-doubt, he would wonder if he made a mistake and whether he ought to go back to his old job. He resented the well-intentioned queries from his friends and family on how his job hunting is going. He longed to enjoy his well-deserved career break without feeling pressured to be earning again. Even doing the things he loved, such as being a DJ, which he never had time for when he was working, had become tinged with anxiety as he wondered if he was right to be "wasting" his precious time in this way.

Sam overcame his fears and anxieties, and worked with me in getting clear on the kind of role that would become a stepping stone to the life he wanted. Within a few months, he got a job heading up the strategy and operations for a young tech startup.

Both Tara and Sam had come to closely associate their self-worth and social standing with what they did for a living. As time passed and their life circumstances changed, there were emotional and physical cues telling them that they needed to do something different. And yet at first their social conditioning and the old ways of thinking were keeping them trapped in the status quo. At times, the fear of losing what they'd worked so hard for was greater than the potential benefits of taking a leap of faith. It took coaching and courage to confront the reality of their situation and make a different choice.

Alka – an MBA who lost her mojo

Alka grew up in a small town in Northern India. The setting was rural and opportunities for higher education were few. From an early age, her main purpose was to make her parents proud and do better than her friends and relatives. Despite the fierce competition, she qualified as an engineer and then went on to do an MBA.

In her reflective moments she can see what a long way she has come from her humble beginnings. And yet, she doesn't feel very confident in corporate settings, and tells me that she no longer feels as ambitious or competitive. Alka knows she is not fulfilling her potential and trailing behind her peers. And yet, the comfort zone has become like quicksand. She feels unable and unwilling to fight or move forward.

She's become aware that she can get emotional very easily and doesn't always know why. Despite having a loving family and supportive friends, she experiences feelings of intense loneliness and inadequacy. She grew up in a family where sharing feelings was not encouraged and her relationship with her parents was a very formal one. She wants emotional support but finds it hard to open up about her feelings. She uses journaling as a way to process and release them.

PART 2

YOU ARE UNIQUE, BUT NOT ALONE

Feeling anxious and stuck in the life you know but no longer love is far more common than you might think. Sam was brave enough to step away from a world that no longer served him, but his conditioning and the response of the people in his ecosystem made him doubt himself. Tara's situation was exacerbated by the fact that there was another life she would have loved to live, being a full-time mother to her young child, but she was fearful that this would be viewed as an "easy option" and damage her self-worth. Alka finds some relief through journaling, but there are layers of trapped emotions her conscious mind is unaware of that may be responsible for her lack of energy and purpose.

The 2022 annual study by the American Institute of Stress provides sobering statistics on the impact of stress on people's lives as well as economic output. They studied people in 143 countries and found that on average 35% reported that they were stressed. The corresponding figure for Americans was 55%. One million Americans miss work each day due to stress and 63% of US workers are ready to quit their jobs to avoid work-related stress.

In his bestselling book *When the Body Says No: The Cost of Hidden Stress* author Dr Gabor Maté says, *"The research literature has identified three factors that universally lead to stress: uncertainty, the lack of information and the loss of control."* He goes on to say, *"Many of us live, if not alone, then in emotionally inadequate relationships that do not recognize or honour our deepest needs. Isolation and stress affect many who may believe their lives are quite satisfactory."*

I would add that the most emotionally inadequate relationship in the vast majority of people's lives is the one they have with themselves. Unless we address that gap, it is unlikely the other relationships in our lives will be as fulfilling as they can be. And it is this yawning gap that is hard to bridge alone. You won't like everything you see, and that is OK. You will come face to face with truths that might make you recoil, or at least feel uncomfortable. That's OK too. Self-love comes from acceptance, warts and all, of *what is* whilst working towards *what can be*.

HOW THIS PROBLEM COMES ABOUT

As mentioned before, our body stores up memories long after our brain has "archived" them. You think your actions are being driven by your mind: the repository of all your conscious knowledge. What's actually happening is that your body has already decided what action you are going to take even before your brain has become aware of it. Most of your daily routines are done in auto-pilot mode that you'd struggle to explain or intellectualise.

Maybe your life is filled with tasks to be done, people to be pleased, responsibilities to be shouldered, deadlines to be met. You look around and see that you're not alone. Stress is everywhere. Some people are even thriving on it and using it to propel themselves forward, calling it "good stress". You don't want to appear weak or lacking in ambition, so you power through, silencing the voice within you and ignoring the signals your body is sending you telling you that all is not well. At its gentlest, this sounds like the pleading of your heart, the warnings from your gut or the whispers of your soul. By the time you're noticing physical symptoms that cause discomfort, pain or worse, your body is literally screaming for your attention.

PART 2

The truth is that even these cries for help from your own body can be drowned out by the noises of the world you live in. Ever heard the expression "no pain, no gain"? It is a world that has conditioned you to buy into certain myths and follow paths that supposedly lead to success and recognition.

The ecosystem you live, work and socialise in plays a huge role in how you cope with the challenges in life. Let's look at the ecosystem you work in as an example. Take a moment to pause and reflect on these questions I invite you to ask yourself about your working life:

Does my working day leave my emotional battery being:

- ☐ *slightly drained, but back to fully charged after a restful night.*
- ☐ *depleted, and not back to full charge even after a downtime at home.*
- ☐ *severely drained and consistently operating on low-power mode.*
- ☐ *fully charged up because I love my work and can't wait to start each day.*

For a follow-up, more probing inquiry, ask yourself:

- What are the activities in my working day that energise me?
- What are the activities in my working day that drain me of energy?
- Which interactions leave me feeling energised?
- Which interactions leave me feeling drained?

A similar reflective exercise on the other ecosystems in your life can also be revealing. The person who chose option 4 in the question above is in a job most people would love to have. However, it is just possible that their responses to the same questions relating to their family life or social circle might be very different. Perhaps they are workaholics, and all their waking hours are spent in that one room of the metaphorical house called life. There is an absence of balance, which is also detrimental to the long-term wellbeing of the person.

What does balance look like in this respect? It's a recognition that there is a duality in most things – a give and take. A gift and a receipt. Some things, people and experiences will fill us with joy, teach us things and bring meaning to our lives. Even experiencing one of those three things is energising. Conversely, there will be times when we are dealing with tasks, situations and people who are demanding, uninteresting and downright draining. These people may be drawing on our energy to fill their depleted reserves.

If you're in the presence of an energy vampire, you may only realise later how exhausted, irritable or even resentful you feel. How do you restore your internal balance? In this book we're going to explore how you can become aware of these dynamics and create strategies that help you stay in balance. We're going to explore ways to identify and uphold your boundaries so you protect yourself from those who drain you of life force and energy.

PART 2

WHY I WROTE THIS BOOK

Remember that question I asked earlier about how your working day made you feel? There was a time when in answer to that question I would have said that I truly loved my job, that it energised me and I couldn't wait to start each new day. I genuinely believed that I was blessed with the best job in the world, and that I was lucky to have a supportive husband who had volunteered to be the stay-at-home parent to our children. I felt grateful, and I felt guilty. I was spending long hours at work doing a job that was intellectually stimulating and rewarding. I felt guilty because I wasn't there to drop off and pick up my kids from school. To an external observer, we were a happy, well-adjusted family. Other women told me how lucky I was when they found out our unusual arrangement and that I always came home after work to a delicious home-cooked meal prepared lovingly by my then husband.

But not everything was as it seemed. In my heart and gut, I sensed something was amiss in my working life, in my marital relationship and the family dynamic. I tried to address it and made compromises, but something was still not right. Our life was comfortable, even joyful, at least on the surface. My kids were in safe hands and my job meant we were financially in a good place; I didn't want to rock the boat. I found myself making adjustments, stepping in to carry more of the load, reframing the negative into positive thoughts, and generally giving in to keep the peace.

In 2014, I was hit by a perfect storm of events. First, my dream job had started to lose its allure due to internal and external factors. I no longer looked forward to my day at work. Second, being a stay-at-home parent to our now older children was no longer a full-time job, nor a fulfilling one for their dad. Boredom and inertia had become a toxic combination. And its effects were having a detrimental impact on our family.

It took a phone call from my daughter's school to shake me out of my complacency. Unbeknownst to me, my beautiful vibrant teenager had been suffering in silence. Her teachers had noticed changes in behaviour that I had been too preoccupied to register. Our family's dysfunctionality had crept up on us slowly but steadily. It took an external observer to propel me out of my comfort zone.

At the end of 2014 I decided to take early retirement. I spent the first year being there for my family, paying attention to the big things and the small things. Especially the small things, because they're the ones that get missed. The things that are clues to a brewing situation that could one day balloon into a giant problem.

I look back on that time now with a mixture of regret and gratitude. Regret, that it took me so long to see what was always there and growing right before my eyes, and gratitude, that I had the courage to finally leap out of my comfort zone into the unknown. In this past decade I have learnt more about myself, human nature and the abundance of the universe than I did in the previous 47 years.

So much of my life's learning has been catalysed by the people who came into my life as teachers, mentors, counsellors and coaches. The challenges and curveballs have been my greatest teachers. Their influence on me has been disproportionately skewed towards the latter part of my life. The learning accelerated when I came to see that asking for help is not a sign of weakness. I have always worn my hard-won self-sufficiency and resilience as an invisible badge of honour. But I could see it made no sense to spend a lifetime trying to figure something out if there was a way to do it faster with a bit of help.

There were times when the uncertainty felt unbearable and the burden seemed too great to bear. As answers to my questions were hard to find in the usual places, I had no choice but to look within and seek guidance. Now that I am at a reasonable distance from that traumatic period in my life, and, dare I say, in a more settled place, I can look back at my two-decade-long corporate career in finance more objectively. It was a good stint and I vastly exceeded my own not particularly high expectations.

If I could go back in time and advise my younger self, there is just one thing I would say to her: don't be too proud to ask for help. Find yourself a good coach or mentor. Someone who will make you feel seen, heard and understood. Someone who will help you see who you truly are and what is possible for you. If you think what you have now is great, you ain't seen nothing yet. Today, I am the coach I wish I'd had in my younger years.

In my quiet moments, I turn to my future self who I imagine being happier, more fulfilled and in her flow. She is the vision of who I want to be. I look at who I am today and ask myself what I need to do to bridge the gap to who I see myself becoming. It begins with taking my backpack off my shoulders and gently placing it on the ground to take stock of what to keep and what to set free.

BECOME THE CREATOR OF YOUR FUTURE

"The best way to predict the future is to create it. Not from the known but from the unknown."

This quote by Dr Joe Dispenza has become the mantra of my life. It is a non-linear approach to life, meaning you don't extrapolate from where you are or expect events to happen in a predetermined sequence. You don't need to get to D via A, B and C. You can explore an infinite number of possible ways to get to D, of which going via A, B and C is only one.

You may have heard of the concept of visioning or future pacing. We will cover this in more detail later in the book. Put simply, you would begin with the end in mind and then work out what you need to do to get there. In our example below, if your desired end point is D then you are going to believe with utter conviction that you will get there. In fact, in your mind's eye, you can see yourself already there. That last bit is particularly important. If you believe something has already happened it leaves no room for doubt or ambiguity. Let me explain how it works with two analogies.

Imagine you decide you want to go travelling but want to go somewhere you've never been before and a place that is not the usual tourist destination. You know you want to go somewhere that is by the sea, where it's warm and the pace is mellow. This narrows your options a little, but the wish is still too wide open and ambiguous.

Now close your eyes and imagine you are already in this dream location. You're on a beach. You are walking barefoot. The sand under your feet is warm and soft. The sea is calm and a stunning aquamarine blue reflecting the sky above which is clear other than for a few wispy clouds. Pay closer attention. What else do you see? When you leave the beach and go into the local town, what language are the locals speaking? How are they towards you? What kind of clothes are the locals wearing? What's the local food like? When you are out on the beach, what's the temperature like? When the sun sets, what colour is the landscape? Does the evening breeze carry any particular fragrance? As the night deepens and you look up at the sky, what do you see? If you can see the stars, how close are they? And so on. With every question, your vision becomes clearer. You see, hear, taste and feel this future reality. You will now more easily be able to identify where in the world this dream destination is and what you need to do in order to go there.

Why does this kind of visioning work? First, the logical explanation with the second of my analogies of a jigsaw puzzle. Let's say there are two teams that are being asked to solve a jigsaw puzzle. The first team is given the pieces of the puzzle without the box with the picture of the finished puzzle on it. The other team is given the same jigsaw puzzle with the box it came in that has the picture on its cover. Which team do you think will solve the puzzle more quickly and easily?

Our future is a highly complex and evolving jigsaw puzzle. Creating it from a place of possibility begins with *not* extrapolating from where you are today. Instead, you must begin by visualising where you want to be, where you see your future self, and believe with absolute conviction that it is where you will be and where you belong.

Knowing what you're working towards, seeing the big picture, will help you to plan better. It will help you to identify the right people, say yes to the right opportunities and focus your efforts in the right direction. Most importantly, it will help you to steer clear of the multitude of possibilities that are simply not right for you.

The second less logical and far more magical explanation for why this works is to do with the energy field. Let's say the universe has a number of possible ways in which your life could turn out. Instead of going on autopilot down an old well-trodden path, you decide to consciously pick one of the more interesting possibilities and energetically position yourself to manifest it. It's like tuning into the right radio station or streaming channel for the kind of programme you're looking for. Tuning into the right frequency to receive what you want is how you can manifest the life you want. But it takes effort, persistence and faith. We will explore all this in a lot more detail.

Creating from a realm of possibility is so much more fun. But it is not easy. The comfort zone is a very seductive place and inertia will flex its impressive muscles. Why would you leave something that is working just fine in pursuit of something that might not work at all? You might also believe that maintaining the status quo is kinder to the people who are in this comfort zone with you. You don't want to be blamed for being a disruptor.

As a catalyst for change, pain is often more powerful than possibility. When we are faced with certain pain, it is tangible and might be happening now. It may be too great to be ignored. We may have no choice other than to take action.

Possibility, on the other hand, is in the future. Possibility might be invisible and mostly in our imagination. It is in our mind and heart, but we may not yet feel its presence in our life. Chasing after a possibility is fraught with uncertainty. It can feel intangible, even unreachable.

There is another risk: what if you get to this new place that you saw in your mind's eye and find that you don't like it? The door to your old life might now be firmly shut. There might be no going back. And even if you were to go back, that which you left behind might not feel the same. Over time, everything changes. You will have changed. Your experience will have changed you. And you will see your old life with a fresh pair of eyes, through the lens of someone who has experienced a new way of being.

WHY WE BECOME PRISONERS OF STATUS QUO

Sometimes our pain is so closely entwined with our life's story that it becomes part of our identity. Who would we be if we walked away from the only life we have ever known? For people who have struggled to be noticed, their pain might be the way they get the attention they so desperately crave. Remember, our body will do what it can to get what it needs, however painful it might be.

The other reason we might persist with a half-life is because the catalyst or inspiration for a different life has not grabbed and held our attention powerfully enough. Life as we know it has a way of keeping us captive.

It doesn't help that in a world that leaves us overstimulated, we all suffer from some level of attention deficit disorder.

Have you ever read a book, listened to a Ted talk or been to a workshop and felt inspired to make a change? How long was it before you realised you'd forgotten most of what you learnt and slid back into old habits?

Ebbinghaus's Forgetting Curve is the result of memory experiments by 19th century German psychologist Hermann Ebbinghaus. He experimented on himself to measure how much information his brain was able to retain and the different ways in which this retention could be improved. Further studies suggest that on average, the human brain forgets 50% of information received within an hour, 70% within 24 hours, and by the end of the week, as much as 90% of what we learned is lost.

Here are a few ways in which we can retain and relive information:

1. **Repeat**. If we see or hear or experience the same things again and again, it sticks in our memory more than things that are transient.

2. **Relate**. When it rhymes and reminds us of events in our own lives it becomes more relevant and meaningful, and hence memorable.

3. **Reshape/Recreate**. When we take what we learn and put it into practice in a way that is right for us, it creates new experiences that help to reshape our current experiences and rewire our brain's existing memories with new ones.

But before we can allow this to happen, we must first overcome the inertia that keeps us stuck. Here are some of the unconscious beliefs and value systems that we inadvertently buy into that hold us back, stopping us from experimenting with, and experiencing, a different way of being.

#1: Wanting more, or wanting something different, makes me ungrateful

This is particularly hard for people who have been brought up to be grateful and always look on the bright side of life. Gratitude is a wonderful thing, but like I said before, it does have a darker side in the form of guilt. This grateful optimist is aware of the extreme hardship in the world and knows how lucky they are compared to most. An absence of happiness isn't something to cry about, right? In their quiet moments they feel a longing for a life not yet lived, for a life that might feel forbidden. Even considering such a life may bring with it feelings of guilt and shame. This is particularly hard when to the outside world their life seems perfect, and their desire for more looks like the self-indulgent whim of a selfish person. The fear of being judged may lead to people living empty lives in gilded cages.

There's a scene in *Downton Abbey* in which Lord Grantham, played by the actor Hugh Bonneville, is saying goodbye to someone who briefly offered him a glimpse of another more carefree life, albeit an adulterous one. She asks, "Will you be happy? Will you?" To which he replies, "I have no right to be unhappy, which is almost the same."

#2: Self-love is vain and narcissistic

In an age of Instagram and the relentless quest for more heart-shaped affirmations, love for oneself has become synonymous with vanity and an unhealthy need for external validation. I had recently finished listening to Kamal Ravikant's audiobook *Love Yourself Like Your Life Depends On It* and had found it a refreshing way to deal with some of the challenges in life. Days later, I was recording a conversation for my podcast with a successful entrepreneur and now a mentor to start ups. He related his life-long habit of having a conversation with himself in the mirror. With a smile, but in all seriousness, I asked him if he said "I love you" to himself during his mirrored monologues. He visibly recoiled at this notion and immediately rubbished that sort of thing as vanity and narcissistic behaviour.

How did self-love become so tainted? Can you love yourself without hubris? Why is it OK to love someone else completely and unconditionally, but somehow you are deemed unworthy of such a gift from yourself? We will explore this in more detail later in the book.

#3: My self-worth is tied up with status, achievement and wealth

The examples of Tara and Sam in an earlier chapter tell you how entrenched this particular myth is in our conditioned behaviour. The things we do have become more important than who we are. It begins from an early age when you notice that the adults around you praise you for doing well at school, for behaving well in social settings, for winning competitions and sporting events. Even well-meaning parents may inadvertently be sending the message that you are loved and deemed worthy when you do well. What happens when the child doesn't meet the parents' expectations? To a child the silent disappointment of a beloved parent can feel more painful than an angry outburst. The withdrawal of love and attention can lead to feelings of sadness and shame, and it can entrench the unconscious belief that they are loved only when they meet or beat the expectations of the people in their lives. What a terrible burden to live with. Can we separate who we are from what we do? What if you knew that you are loved irrespective of what you do and how much you achieve? How would that change the way you view yourself?

#4: Asking for help signifies weakness and makes me a victim

I know this well from personal experience. I grew up in a family that prized self-sufficiency and independence. My parents' unwritten rule was that my brother and I had full autonomy when it came to our education and our career choices. That way our successes were ours alone and any failures could not be blamed on anyone else. I am very grateful for my upbringing, which made me a resilient and self-sufficient person. But I also grew up with a belief that even though my parents loved me and wanted what was best for me, they would not have my back, and that I had better learn to fight my own battles.

I realise now that asking for help is a muscle. The more you use it, the better it works. And like any muscle, overuse or the wrong use has consequences of weakening other muscles. I hated asking for help, because by the time I did, I had exhausted all my own reserves to help myself and I was desperate. At that point, being turned down felt like a body blow rejection that reaffirmed my belief that it was not a good idea to ask for help.

As I look back on my life, I can see the many occasions when I soldiered on through the challenges on my solitary march believing no one could help me. Of course, through my hardships, I grew stronger. But I also wasted time, and I didn't give people who wanted to help a chance to do so. Now I am in a helping profession myself, I can see what a struggle it can be for people who are like how I once was.

#5: I have to earn my place in this world

This is an offshoot of myth number 3. What happens to people who don't have the external validation of their worth in the form of social status or a job title or financial independence? What happens to someone who grows up with an emotionally unavailable primary carer? The message the child might take away is that the only way to get their attention is to take care of the parent's physical or emotional needs, by working hard and doing things that will make them happy. In patriarchal societies, girls are often brought up believing that they must learn to be carers, nurturers and homemakers. They may grow up feeling responsible for meeting the non-financial needs of the family as a wife, daughter-in-law and mother. Unlike the person who has a paid job as a means to feel worthy, this woman's need is even more basic. She may believe she must earn the right to belong.

This is at the heart of why some people become life-long givers. They become so attuned to other people's wants and needs that they can anticipate your needs before you know you have them. They routinely put other people's needs and desires ahead of their own. On the face of it, this is a wonderful, selfless quality, one that is so admired as a human virtue. This belief runs so deep within the human psyche, particularly amongst women, that even when she is highly gifted, successful and financially independent, she may live with a deep-seated fear of not having "earned" her place and therefore fears being found out. This is often described as the Imposter Syndrome. Deep down she believes that she doesn't deserve the gifts life has given her and she must work hard to keep them and prepare for a time when it might all be taken away from her. Instead of feeling grateful for all that life has given her, she may instead be wracked with a misplaced guilt that plagues her very existence.

How many of these traits do you recognise in yourself? Greater self-awareness is the first big step towards change. Often, even that is not enough. Let's reiterate why we stay when going makes sense. There are some very understandable reasons why the majority choose to stick to the status quo, stay in their comfort zone, even after it no longer feels very comfortable. You might relate to one or more of these.

- Stepping into the unknown is scary and there's no certainty you'll like what you find. And then what if you can't get back to what you have now? Better the devil you know!

- You've become used to quick fixes and instant gratification. Upsetting the status quo might be unpopular, take much longer and be hard work. You're not sure you have the time or the energy for it.

- The costs of embarking on this journey of change are relatively certain but the benefits are not. Some outcomes are intangible and hard to quantify. How are you meant to measure the value of happiness or freedom or better health? You don't know how to assess whether it will be worth it.

- Your way of life with all its flaws has become a big part of your identity. Who will you be if you replace those aspects of your life with something else?

- If you succeed in creating the life you see in your mind's eye, you will have to walk away from the life you now know, including the people who are your clan and make up your ecosystem. You're not sure you're ready to let go.

LEARNING TO LET GO: ANAMIKA'S STORY

Anamika's life changed when she suffered a significant setback in her health. It forced her to slow down and notice what was really going on inside her. She recalls the time when she first experienced the power of letting go. *"I was in the hospital with an impacted spleen. A friend conveyed a spiritual message telling me to simply let go. When I reflected on this message, I realised how much I was holding on to and how it was affecting me from within. I let go of baggage, I learnt what my limiting beliefs were. Now, I journal, I reflect, I make changes, I see threads and I let go."*

Anamika has always been curious, looking for opportunities to learn, know and experience life. Resilience is one of her strong traits. She prides herself for being able to bounce back, not wallow in self-pity or in any other "non-serving emotion".

Emotional baggage and limiting beliefs were not the only things Anamika learned to let go. *"I've been learning to let go of the illusion of control. Instead, I focus on the now, on what I can do and what is in my control. Connection has become particularly important to me since my illness. True connection comes from deep silence, deep listening, deep love and non-judgmental acceptance."*

She admits that the negative emotion she most often experiences is hurt. *"I wish I could have greater emotional equanimity. Often I don't know where the hurt is coming from. When it happens my default reaction is to shout. When I realise I am shouting, I move myself out of the situation and retreat to be alone. That way I get away from the trigger. Expressing myself was very important to me; today, I no longer believe it is essential that I communicate everything I feel and think."*

Anamika says, *"I am thankful for my cancer experience and view it as a springboard to my personal development. My greatest learning about myself is that I can do whatever is required of me. That I will always find ways to make it happen. I have also developed a healthy relationship with money. My life is devoted to helping people, but that does not conflict with making money to take care of my needs."*

TURNING UNCONSCIOUS REACTIONS INTO CONSCIOUS RESPONSES

Unexplained negative feelings are particularly hard to deal with because your conscious mind has no idea why you are feeling this way. If you're someone who can't bear to show weakness or vulnerability, the sadness, hurt and disappointment might be expressed in more forceful ways, such as by verbally lashing out at people who had nothing to do with those feelings.

Part of our personal growth is finding the balance between processing and expressing the emotions we feel with awareness and consideration for how our expression affects others. If you grew up in a household where there was a lot of freely expressed anger, it will undoubtedly have affected you and how you process emotions in adulthood.

The awareness of our emotional reactions to triggering events is a powerful first step. Viktor Frankl, author of *Man's Search For Meaning* talks about the space between stimulus and response. He says, *"In that space is our power to choose our response. In our response lies our growth and freedom."*

Isolating and moving away from the offending trigger can help, but there is a risk that this behaviour morphs into conflict avoidance. Walking away to create space and assess your response is healthy if it is accompanied by acknowledgement and acceptance of how the triggering event made you feel. Once you are truly aware of those feelings, they can be processed and released. And then it is possible to reframe your response to one that is more appropriate and productive.

PART 2

As you evolve into the person you are meant to be, you will let go of old trapped emotions, people, places and things that no longer belong in your life. That process of letting go is necessary if you are to create space for new connections and fresh opportunities. You must also learn to recognise, process, express, release and reframe all kinds of emotions on an ongoing basis. This prevents unhealthy emotions from becoming trapped once again.

Like a hoarder who has just cleared out years of accumulated junk, you must avoid falling back into unhelpful old hoarding habits. This is not easy. Opening a door to things you've ignored for years is daunting. The feeling of spaciousness and freedom that comes after a major decluttering exercise can feel just as overwhelming.

The process of transformation is anything but comfortable. You only have to look at the process of a caterpillar morphing into a butterfly. If the caterpillar knew becoming a butterfly would be such a violent process of self-annihilation, it might not choose to transform. Luckily for us butterfly lovers, the caterpillar doesn't know and has no choice.

The good news is we don't all have to aim for transformation. Conscious evolution is enough. What's needed is a desire for change and a willingness to co-create it. Change is happening within us and around us whether we like it or not. Why not take greater control of the changes by introducing greater awareness and intentionality? The small changes compound over time and could well lead to transformative results.

PART 3

PART 3

I remember a scene from the film *How Do You Know* where Reese Witherspoon's character has discovered she's been unceremoniously dropped from her baseball team. She's popular in a bubbly, kind, team-spirited, girl-next-door kind of way. The news is a shock to her and her teammates. To help her overcome this setback she goes to a therapist. After only a few minutes on the therapist's couch she changes her mind and heads for the door saying that she's fine, and she doesn't need therapy. As she's about to leave, she pauses and asks the therapist what is the one most helpful general piece of advice he'd give anyone. To which he says, "figure out what you want and learn how to ask for it". She thinks about this for a few seconds and then says, "they're both really hard".

For many of us we stumble at the very first step. Knowing what you want with crystal clarity is hard. It is far easier to make a long list of things you don't like or don't want. But when people are asked to articulate in a simple sentence what they really, really want, most are stumped. Have you noticed people who know what they want and very often get it with seemingly effortless ease?

WHY WE DON'T ALWAYS KNOW WHAT WE REALLY WANT

From a very young age we become attuned to the people and the world around us. How we are treated by those entrusted with our care, how they and other authority figures behave, what they believe in, how they respond to adversity and opportunity, all influence our own attitudes and values. At school we're taught, sometimes forced, to conform. We wear uniforms and are encouraged to blend in. We follow a prescribed set of rules and are punished when we deviate from them. Standing out draws unwelcome attention.

Don't be so loud, don't be so dramatic, don't be so proud! Don't disobey, don't talk back, don't show off, don't daydream, don't dress that way, don't, don't, don't!! My mother recalls having a growth spurt in her third grade and suddenly becoming the tallest in her class. This caused her great embarrassment, especially as strangers would assume she was older. Don't be so tall, was the unspoken message she took away. It seeded a lifelong habit of slouching to make herself smaller. And with that one little habit she diminished her perception of herself for the rest of her life.

As children we take away messages that shape our behaviours and influence our personalities. Well-meaning parents might be aghast to discover how their actions and words, designed to help and protect, were interpreted by their child's fertile mind.

A parent who pushes their child to study hard and top their class is doing so because they want the best for their child. When the child succeeds, they might lavish them with praise and attention. When the child's results are less than stellar, they might show their disappointment in ways that makes the child believe that they are loved only when they do well and achieve things. They might go on to unconsciously need external validation to feel good enough or wanted. Such children often grow up to become hyper competitive or even workaholics.

Another example is a parent who is emotionally unavailable. They're too caught up in their own emotional turmoil to pay any attention to their child. The child learns to read the parent's moods and do things and behave in ways that might elicit some positive emotion from the parent. Such children might take away the message that they are only loved and noticed when they do things to please others. As adults they may go on to become "givers" and people pleasers.

Children who feel loved only when they are "good" or when they do the right thing may go on to become perfectionists and/or live with this strong feeling of responsibility. They might have a strong inner critic: a voice that reminds them of their critical parent who was quick to berate, slow to praise.

Children who were overpowered by a controlling parent who made them feel unsafe might grow into adults who find it hard to drop their guard, to be vulnerable, even with loved ones. Such adults often become protective of the weak and bullied, and they may have anger issues when they feel they're being controlled.

Children who were demeaned or bullied may discover the power of making people laugh, becoming a class clown, as a way to mitigate the threat. As adults they might continue to use humour and variety as a way to escape being stuck in monotony or deep emotions.

When we can see someone as they once were, and take time to see the world through the eyes of the child they once were, we might understand why they are the way they are. This compassionate understanding can be very healing and pave the way to a different way of behaving.

Most rules are designed to maintain structure, keep the peace, exert control and limit dissonance. Can you imagine a school with hundreds of children running riot doing what they like and being exactly who they want to be? There would be chaos. They'd grow up thinking only of their own needs and desires. They'd learn none of the niceties of living in civilised society. Or at least that is the perceived wisdom. It is true that children need some structure and find routines comforting. But if we're not careful, that initial bending of the will leads to a suppression of all that makes the child unique.

Not every education system stifles curiosity and creativity, and there are many excellent teachers out there who nurture children so they blossom into the adults they have the potential to be, but the vast majority of education systems around the world are designed to prepare students for tests and qualifications. They focus on academic success, not on developing the tools needed to live an abundant life.

Once they emerge from the education system, they enter the world of work where they are required to prove their worth. After a decade or more of learning to conform and compete, they are now being asked to demonstrate how they stand out amongst others who have similar or better qualifications.

In a world where every individual is unique, and portraying your uniqueness and personal brand is a thing, they might not know what makes them stand out in ways that are positive. They will compete within a framework they know, using strategies they've grown up with, and aiming to be better than everyone else. With that will begin a race to a finish that doesn't really ever end.

PART 3

The competition is fierce. It can be disheartening when you realise that what you've learnt through formal education has not prepared you for the real world. You've mastered the theory of how to swim, at best paddling in the shallow end of the pool with a floor and walls to keep you safe. Now you're having to navigate a deep, choppy and ever-changing sea with no one to show you the way. Everyone else is also swimming to stay afloat and it is truly the survival of the fittest.

YOUR INNER WORLD AND YOUR OUTER WORLD

Navigating your inner world is about greater self-awareness. It's about developing tools and strategies to connect and communicate with yourself. It's about gaining clarity: getting to know yourself as an individual – who you are, why you are the way you are, what you do, why you do it, how you do it, and so on.

Navigating the outer world is about how you show up in the world. The places and the people. The problems and the opportunities. The everyday stimuli that trigger reactions from you. How you show up and interact with it all. You often hear people say, "Just be yourself!" What does this really mean? Who and what really am I? Can I really be the same me irrespective of the circumstances and ecosystem? Which self is the real me and which self is the right one for this occasion?

THE FIRST STEP IS SELF-AWARENESS

"I was ashamed of myself when I realised life is a costume party and I attended with my real face."

FRANZ KAFKA

"Being yourself" in a world that may not be ready for your unadulterated authenticity has its pitfalls. You may not fit in with the norm. There is a risk of being ridiculed, ostracised, or even banished. The need to belong, to be seen and accepted, is a deep human need. Which is why part of our early learning is to develop antennas that pick up signals telling us what we need to do and who we need to be in order to feel safe, loved and accepted.

The problem arises when we live our lives on this basis, being and doing what we think others want us to be and do. We may go through life never really knowing who we are beneath all those masks we wear, never knowing what we really want.

Going inwards can help you connect with your true self. This is the *"you"* who is hidden behind all the masks you wear. These masks keep you safe in a world where you've learned that not everyone has your best interests at heart.

Different aspects of your true self are revealed depending on where you are, who you're with and why you're there. Understanding these various aspects of your true self is an important part of your self-awareness because they mingle with the persona you choose to present to the world.

PART 3

The same you is presented slightly differently depending on whether you're at work in a client meeting, at home cooking dinner for the family, with friends celebrating a birthday, or on holiday enjoying some much-deserved downtime.

William James, in his book *The Principles of Psychology*, puts it beautifully when he says, "A man has as many social selves as there are individuals who recognise them."

Like the clothes in your wardrobe. You might wear a smart business suit when you're meeting a client. You're unlikely to wear that to the gym. There will be a different set of clothes for when you're lounging around at home watching TV or when you're out meeting friends. Each of these sets of clothes serve a purpose and are designed to match the occasion. When you have a really good sense of what shape, style, type of fabric, colours and designs really suit you, your clothes will become an extension of who you are. People then notice you, not the clothes you wear.

It is the same with these masks we wear. It is unrealistic and unsafe to go through life revealing our every vulnerability. It's the equivalent of walking around with no clothes on. Instead, what if we become so comfortable in our skin, so certain or sanguine about our place in the world, that even our masks become a part of who we are. Like the outer layers of an onion. They protect and preserve our inner sanctum whilst still being authentically true to us.

THE ROLE OF UPBRINGING IN THE DEVELOPMENT OF PERSONALITY

Our attitudes and behaviour as adults is a product of our childhood experiences, the beliefs and values of our ecosystem and the role models we grow up with. Below are a few examples of how upbringing plays a role in how personality traits are developed and how they shape the way we show up in the world.

Divya

Divya grew up in a small town in India. She says, *"I had big dreams and believed I could really be something. My mum was a hard worker and my dad was a dreamer who lived life king-sized. I was very close to my father and was very pampered."*

When Divya was only 12 years old, her father unexpectedly died. *"When my father passed away at the beginning of my seventh grade, I didn't consciously decide anything. I don't remember being sad. I simply found out what needed to be done and did it. I took on the responsibility of being a big sister and moved out of childhood almost overnight."*

Only years later did Divya realise that as a child she never processed the loss of her beloved father. Therapy helped her go back to her 12-year-old self, connect the dots and grieve. It also helped her see that deep down she blamed her mother for this loss.

This long-suppressed sadness and grief meant that the negative emotion she experienced most was anger and it was the people closest to her, the ones she loved, who bore the brunt of it. *"I used to get angry with my mum over small things. I couldn't accept I was wrong or say sorry. I was never like that with my friends. My relationship with her is so much better now. The emotions I feel lately that I still don't understand are sadness and betrayal."*

She now attributes this trying time in her life for her people-pleasing tendencies. *"Many of my life's decisions were driven by that. If I had my time again, I'd have made bolder choices. I can also see how I went through life feeling not enough, and hence I pushed myself to excel in order to be good enough for people. Deep down, I don't care about the things people think I care about. I care about my heart being taken care of. There's a feeling of longing for a kind of love that shows that I matter. I know I am loved, but I question the way I am loved. I feel best when I'm with my dog from whom I feel zero judgement."*

Madhu

Madhu's journey to self-discovery and resilience began early, when at the age of five she was diagnosed with muscular dystrophy.

"Everything was slower for me. I would get very angry at not being on par with the other kids, especially physically. I questioned life and how things would be for me later in life." She credits her mother for instilling her with self-belief. *"My mother was very sure that I would get through it all because of my resilience. She saw what I could be, and that made me believe in me and shaped me as a person. She drilled into me the importance of being financially independent. I became confident without being unnecessarily sympathetic towards myself."* Madhu and her siblings

were encouraged to make their own decisions and take full responsibility for them no matter what the consequences.

Madhu grew up in a "blunt family full of girls" where talking about feelings, the rights and wrongs of the world, was unfiltered and normal. She says, *"We were vocal and were given a free space where our points of view were heard and accepted by our parents. When we went to visit family and friends, we learnt to adopt a different tone depending on who we were with."* This is a great example of a child being taught early on that freedom of speech must be tempered with an awareness of the appropriateness of such candour.

Authenticity and honesty are very important to Madhu. *"I have a strong association with honesty. It is important and necessary for me. I can't make meaningful conversations without it. I feel personally disrespected and unsafe without it. Of course, I understand that there can be grey areas, not everything is black or white. I wish I could be more understanding and tolerant of grey areas. I recognise everyone has greys. I want to be more forgiving, and I am making progress, no longer hating people whom I have let go."*

When a person grows up believing their weakness might make them vulnerable, potentially turning them into a victim, being strong and vigilant can become the default mode. This is also true of children who are rewarded for their strength and resilience. They may grow up viewing most things as black or white, right or wrong, you're either with us or against us.

"I use my gut instinct to navigate the outer world. I can just look at someone and know if I can trust them. The people in my inner circle know a version of me that is rebellious,

unapologetic and not seeking validation. In the workplace, I overcompensate and can be viewed as meek and willing to be moulded. I seek ways to maximise how I use my energy. This means I often take the path of least resistance when I know I can't win a battle."

Growing up in a household where no topic was taboo and no emotion too big, Madhu is aware of and processes a range of emotions. *"Anger is the emotion I most frequently experience. Generally, it's because something isn't how I want it to be. I can be bad tempered and unable to measure my words when I'm angry. I don't suppress negative emotions. I am more likely to suppress positive emotions, especially in the face of someone else's unhappiness."*

Vidya

Vidya lost her father suddenly and unexpectedly when she was only 15. This had grave financial consequences for her family, and she believes it is one of the reasons why she became very risk averse.

She says, *"I want to do too many things and that stands in the way of my mental peace."* People who are extremely risk averse find it difficult to embark on any project without having a great deal of certainty and control.

Another way this risk aversion plays out for Vidya is through her quest for knowledge, her love of reading and doing research. She went to an Arya Samaj school and she believes it helped her think about religion and life in a very different way. The Arya Samaj principles are based on the practical interpretation of the Vedic scriptures.

Vidya considers herself to be a mix of extrovert and introvert. She says, *"I am curious and like meeting people, but it takes me time to warm up and really be myself. I engage with people who know more than me."*

She is more comfortable with intellectual pursuits than physical ones. *"When it comes to a physical challenge, I have a deep fear and mental block. If it's a walk or hike, I will do it if there is someone with me. I like controlling things. When I feel control slipping away, I feel very uncomfortable."*

Feelings, emotions and human interactions take up energy. A risk averse person might be very choosy and careful about how they expend their precious energy. They are also likely to spend more time in their own heads (which is a safer place and where they can be in control), so much so that they think about their emotions rather than actually allowing them to be felt. This can lead to avoiding situations that are likely to spark an emotional response, or to interact with people who are prone to emotional outbursts.

"I spend a lot of time thinking about events and my reactions to them," she says. *"Anger is the negative emotion I most often experience. If I don't deal with it, I tend to think about it post facto. For this reason, I prefer to either distance myself or close the loop."*

She goes on to say, *"I want to manage my anger better. I do it much better at work than I do in my personal life, where I take people for granted. I wish I could pause before I talk. It might help me slow down and respond differently."*

Being able to openly express our emotions, particularly negative ones, is a sign that you feel safe. The safety comes from knowing that you are with people who allow you to be your unvarnished, warts-and-all self, without fear of being judged or abandoned. This is unconditional love: the purest and the most life-affirming kind that is most often taken for granted. We must find a way to express how we really feel without making the people closest to us feel like they are our punching bag.

BECOMING A MONK – SILENCE, SPACE AND STILLNESS

Spending time alone, in stillness and silence, can be very powerful. Meditation and mindfulness are proven ways to feel calmer and more present. It isn't the only way. Any activity in which you become completely present and focused on the thing you are doing can feel like meditation. For about ten years, hula-hooping and dance was my moving meditation. I could get lost in the music and become one with my hula-hoop. You can have the same effect when walking in nature, swimming, singing, painting, or playing an instrument or sport.

I first glimpsed the true power of meditation when a few years ago I went on a ten-day silent retreat called Vipassana. I was experiencing a great deal of inner turmoil. This felt like a healthy way to escape the life that was making me so unhappy. In a tranquil place sequestered from the outside world, for the first nine days, my fellow meditators and I had a taste of living like a monk. Regimented mealtimes of small portions of delicious vegetarian food. 10-12 hours of meditation with breaks in between. No talking.

No non-verbal communication, not even eye contact. And definitely no contact with the outside world. Our phones and other personal devices were surrendered at the outset. Not even old fashioned pen and paper were allowed. Any journaling would have to wait.

It was the hardest thing I have physically experienced since I gave birth to my children. It was also one of the most rewarding. At first, it was impossible to quiet the mind. Focusing on my breath was meant to help me guide my attention away from busy thoughts. Being an objective observer of my breath and how it travelled up my nostrils and back out was mind-numbingly dull. I began to wonder if I would last even the first day, let alone ten days. Sitting cross legged on the floor hour after hour, albeit with many cushions and blankets, was more physically demanding than I had ever imagined.

Then on day three something shifted inside me. I was no longer just observing my breath. I was experiencing it. I wasn't just noticing its predictable in and out – I was becoming one with it. My mind cleared and I started to see an image that was so clear, so vivid in its colours and also completely still. Like a gorgeously painted curtain in front of a stage. Even when I opened my eyes and closed them again, it was still there. I later interpreted this as a little sign that there was more to come behind that curtain, but I was not ready to see it yet.

On day four, I became aware of new sensations as my attention scanned my whole body from top of the crown down to every little toe. I felt my hair follicles stir. I felt the weight of my hair that was splayed on my shoulders. As my attention moved to my cheek, I felt a tingling in the exact place where my attention had rested. It was unbelievably thrilling to explore my being from within in this way.

PART 3

As I carried on with this inner exploration, another strange thing happened. I noticed pain and discomfort. Of course, sitting still had something to do with it. My limbs were not accustomed to being in the folded position for such extended periods of time. But more importantly, noticing the sensation made the sensation more pronounced. It was like parts of my inner self were waking up to the fact that I was now paying attention, and they were clamouring to hold on to it. The trick was to notice, acknowledge and move on. The lesson was one of impermanence. This feeling, this sensation, this delight, this agony, it is all transient. Don't let it hold you. Don't hold on to it.

Day ten was when we were finally allowed to speak, to share our experience with others and to acclimatise ourselves to the real world we would soon be going back to. After nine days of silence the sudden return of sound was jarring to my senses. Having been alone with my thoughts, my feelings, my innermost world of sensations, I slightly resented this assault on my senses. The rare feeling of equanimity the nine days had brought me was steadily ebbing away. By the time I had arrived back home it disappeared altogether. Life in its full technicolour chaotic drama awaited me. And I had to show up and deal with it.

That ten-day experience showed me why some people choose to live an isolated hermit-like existence. Some become modern-day monks as an escape from a life that is too overwhelming for them. There is a certain appeal to living a compassionately regimented routine where you don't have to interact with the challenges and uncertainties of everyday life. A life where your basic needs are limited and are taken care of by someone else. In a world that prizes freedom and choice, some find the absence of both blissful and instead choose a simpler life. Some might even prefer the hardship and poverty of a spiritually rich but regimented life to the opulence and turbulence of a "normal" life.

LIFE IS A STAGE – THE ROLE OTHERS PLAY

"All the world's a stage, and all the men and women merely players. They have their exits and their entrances; and one man in his time plays many parts." The quote from Shakespeare's *As You Like It* reminds us that life is like an elaborate stage on which we each have a part to play.

Unlike a theatre performance that is thoroughly rehearsed and predictable, life is more like an unscripted improvisation. Awareness of who we are, how capable (or not) we are, and what we are meant to be doing is important. Equally important is how we show up day after day, how we interact with others, how we deal with curveballs and how we take action even in the face of all the uncertainty.

You are unique and at the core your essence stays the same. However, your persona and your sense of self will constantly evolve as you interact with the world around you. This is why you can never really know who you are until you have got off your meditation mat and experienced life.

Darshana

Darshana is a cheerful, strong-willed woman who admits she can't sit with her own thoughts, that she needs others to see herself more clearly. She adds, *"I'm not good at discovering myself by myself. I always see better when I look at myself through someone else's eyes. When I talk to someone,*

I collate my thoughts better. If I'm feeling upset, I know why I'm feeling that way. What is lacking is the ability to articulate it, especially in intimate relationships. My best friend has played a great role, acting as my mirror, my moral compass."

Having someone in our life who truly sees us and is willing to create a safe space for us is a gift. Being able to articulate in words or actions what's going on in our heart and mind is such an invaluable aspect of processing and expressing thoughts and feelings that would otherwise fester inside us.

This external approach, the reliance on another, requires courage and a willingness to trust and be vulnerable. It comes more easily when you've had people in your life who have been worthy of your trust. Someone who listens well, who doesn't judge, who can be objective as well as empathetic, who offers advice only when you have asked for it, who will not share your secrets nor betray you in some other way.

It is a lot to ask for. And I can tell you from experience, the people who love us most dearly and have our best interests at heart are not always best placed to comply with all of the above, or at least not all of the time. They might be too close to us; too emotionally invested in our wellbeing to be truly objective.

Besides, it is a lot of pressure for one person to become the repository of all our secrets, to always show up in exactly the way we need them to, when we need them. Would we have it in us to be that person for someone all of the time? When the trusted person cracks or disappoints, we may feel utterly betrayed and abandoned.

Darshana found a way to mitigate this risk. She says, *"I used to think I was very independent. A few years ago, I realised that I am emotionally dependent. Not on a single individual, but on multiple individuals. Because they're human beings and might not always be there, it is a high-risk strategy. I have diversified the risk by having a network of friends and confidants. Whenever something disturbs me, I have my helpline: my best friend and my support network of multiple people for different issues. It is important to not rely on one person for everything. I have different people with whom I discuss different issues. For deep stuff and family issues it's my best friend whom I have known for half my life."*

I like her strategy. I am reminded of the African proverb: it takes a village to raise a child. There is a child inside every one of us – the child we once were who lives on no matter how old we are. Our inner child is the embodiment of our deepest and most visceral feelings. We must learn to create our own tribe to help us when times get tough and the child in us seeks comfort or support.

KNOWING WHAT YOU WANT AND ASKING FOR IT

Steve Jobs, the late founder of Apple, famously said, "Most people never ask, and that's what separates the people who do things from the people who just dream about them."

The reluctance to ask and to receive might be tied in with social conditioning and values. If you have a scarcity mindset, you might view receiving as a zero sum game: I receive, therefore someone somewhere is going without. Or you might not like feeling indebted to the giver and not feel ready to part with what they (might) want in exchange.

Getting clear on what we want, why we want it and what we are prepared to do in order to get it helps avoid misunderstandings and potential conflict. When there is abundance, giving and receiving is simply a matter of flow. The giver and the receiver know that their needs will always be met when they express it. And crucially, they understand that giving and receiving does not have to be transactional. It will flow where it needs to go.

Rajul

Rajul has the poise and confidence of an influencer who knows what she wants and is not afraid to ask for it. *"I've always been very vocal about what I want, be it within my family or my career. You could say I'm shameless about asking for what I want. I see it as taking ownership and being true to yourself."*

It is a life skill to be able to clearly identify and articulate what you want. It seems simple enough, and yet most people struggle with this. Consider your own life. If you were to make a list of things you really want, and another list of all the things you don't want or want changed, which would be easier to write? Which list is longer and has greater conviction behind it?

What we want and need might of course change over time. Managing expectations is another crucial aspect of minimising conflict and disappointment.

Rajul says, *"For me, the process of self-discovery has come with the realisation that I have changed over time. The one constant is being true to myself and others, and this results from having clarity of expectations from myself and from others. I'm rebellious and don't believe in following a path set out by others. Understanding my own strengths and weaknesses has been helpful."*

Having supportive parents who allow you the autonomy to make your own choices and the space to make mistakes plays a big role in replenishing the pot of self-belief we are all born with. It makes it so much easier to tread purposefully out into the big wide world, knowing what you want and courageously going after it.

At the age of 21, Rajul decided she wanted laser eye surgery because she didn't like how wearing glasses made her look and feel. Her parents and other well wishers tried to talk her out of a procedure that they feared was risky. Rajul was undeterred by these cautionary voices and was willing to take a calculated risk. She says, *"I did my research, figured out exactly what I was going in for and then persuaded my parents who only wanted what was best for me. That decision catapulted my confidence."*

Sometimes confidence rests on an illusion of control – the ability to be in control, and more importantly to not be controlled by others. Anger was, and still is, a familiar emotion for Rajul. She says, *"Typically, anger would be ignited when people would disagree with me or cast doubt on my decisions. The intensity of my anger would creep up, especially when I couldn't control things. It took me a while to see that there are always perspectives other than mine, and that I have to learn to understand them too. I realised how my anger was negatively impacting my relationships and that I needed to mellow."*

Recognising what is and what isn't in our control is an important step towards navigating difficult situations. Rajul recalls a time when she was in a serious relationship that was going nowhere because the boy's family didn't approve of her. She was angered and hurt by her boyfriend's inability or unwillingness to stand up for her and their relationship. After a year of trying to break the impasse, she finally accepted that how his parents viewed her was outside her control. She made peace with it and let go. Later the boy's parents changed their minds about her but by then she had already moved on and had no wish to go back. She says, *"I learnt a great lesson from that time. I understood the healing power of time, and that things do get better and with time comes greater clarity."*

Now Rajul's self-confidence is tempered with humility, and it serenely sits alongside social and emotional intelligence. She is empathetic and socially aware. *"I do have different personas and I see that as an important part of navigating the outer world,"* she says. *"At work and in my career I am assertive and confident. I am a very different person when I'm with my in-laws, for instance. They treat me like their daughter and mostly care about how much I love their son. They're aware of my different personas, and they know what my true essence is and what my values are."*

Reflecting on our experiences: the impact they've had on us and the impact we've had on the world around us is a powerful way to consciously evolve and grow. Receiving and giving feedback, especially that which highlights uncomfortable truths can really help us and others view events from multiple perspectives.

This is where coaching can be helpful. A coach will hold a mirror up to you and help you see yourself as you've never before. More importantly, a coach will help you see the good in you that you might have long ignored whilst on an endless quest to overcome limitations.

CLIENT STORY - JYOTSNA: FINDING BALANCE AND FULFILMENT

I met Jyotsna back in 2019. She wanted coaching to improve her leadership skills and deal with the sudden changes in her workplace that had made her feel lost and unsure of herself.

In the course of our work together, I'd helped Jyotsna see herself with a fresh pair of eyes and imagine a life of balance, harmony and fulfilment. Over the next few sessions, there were several "Aha!" moments for Jyotsna. She learned to slow down and take time to notice the things that really mattered to her. She became more present both in her personal and professional life. She really listened and learned to exercise greater empathy. Most importantly, she became more present to herself and became aware of what she really wanted.

It was four years later that I met her again when she came forward to help me with this book. I noted how much calmer and more self-assured she looked. There was a glow of contentment that comes from a place of deep self-knowing and acceptance.

She said, *"Before I worked with you, I was not very self-aware. With your life-as-a-house approach, I learned to see what I really wanted and needed to go after. It led me to pursuing hobbies, feeling more at peace and closer to where I want to be. Now I take time to have conversations with myself and ask myself what I really want."*

She realised that what she thought she wanted in life, particularly from her career, were not the things that would create the happy, fulfilled and abundant life she had envisioned in our early sessions. She now values and cherishes time with her family, in particular her young children. Work no longer dominates her life, and knowing what she wants has helped her go after her professional goals with greater clarity and confidence.

When asked more broadly what has helped her in life to get to where she is now, she says, "*What helped me get to where I am was being financially independent. It afforded me the luxury of thinking differently and exploring any gaps. In 2019, when I started working with you, I was two years away from paying off my home loan and had financial stability.*"

In her journey of self-discovery, Jyotsna learned that one of her superpowers was her ability to let things go if they no longer belonged with her or didn't feel right. She has a deep conviction that she has the capability to rebuild and start again. This resilience has been a result of being self-sufficient from an early age.

Jyotsna has had a lifetime's experience of dealing with situations and ecosystems that are new, unfamiliar and challenging. "*When I was growing up, I had to set my own path and chose not to go down the path others wanted me to take. This included my decision to enter higher education and my choice of life partner. I believe I was helped by the fact that my family did not have a high social status and I didn't have an inheritance that would have come with its own baggage of expectations. I was known for myself and by my name, not by my father's name (as my father's daughter). This gave me independence from an early age, unlike some of my cousins who still feel trapped by expectations."*

She admits that what she finds most challenging is set ups that are disorganised and constantly changing. *"I am facing this as my children are growing up and everything keeps changing. I don't have a social circle as I didn't have time for it. Now I crave social connections. I find I am socially awkward and not good with parties and talking to strangers. Social media has reduced 1-1 interactions."*

She confesses to having moments of self-doubt, especially in the social arena. *"I admire women who become the centre of attention at parties. I think maybe I'm not interesting enough; I feel I only know about my work, and not much else."*

Jyotsna found success in a fiercely competitive male-dominated insurance industry, and has now created a more balanced, more fulfilled life for herself. She may be a work-in-progress, but the progress she has made is testament to what is possible when we are willing to go after what we want, embrace change and courageously deal with challenges.

UNCONDITIONAL LOVE

As I sit here today
In the quiet of my mind
To the sound of music
That takes me back in time.

I see a little girl
She's likely two or three
As I look more closely
I realise it's me!

In that instant I know
What's brought me here today
My heart is welling up
With things I need to say.

She, this girl who's me
Knows not what lies ahead
The moments she will treasure
And those she'll soon forget.

The twists and turns
The joy and fears
Excitement and laughter
Mixed with love and tears

All this is yet to come
I mustn't say much more
Have courage and faith, dear one
Know that you're here to grow.

Sweet child, my love
I am the future you
You live inside of me
And divinity lives in you.

For my own peace of mind
There are things I need to say
You might not understand
But please listen anyway.

I'm sorry, for all the times
I left you far behind
Forgot you, ignored you
Belittled you in my mind.

I love you, I always will
A feeling so deep and chaste
In it you'll find the universe
And all who are in its embrace.

Please forgive me,
For not seeing your pain
For denying you joy
Putting you in chains.

Thank you for not giving up
For your patience and trust in me
For accepting my imperfections
And loving me unconditionally.

PART 4

The 7 C's to an Abundant Life

Clarity
Communication
Conflict   Creativity

Competence   Connection
Curiosity

BRINGING YOU THE 7C'S

I created the framework of the 7C's back in 2017 as a common sense guide to navigating your inner world and the outer world. It is designed to help you gain greater clarity of *who you are, what makes you unique and how you can create an abundant life while making a difference in the world.*

In my coaching practice and workshops I met people with a range of objectives. Some wanted greater clarity of their vision, purpose and goals. Some wanted to understand why despite "having it all" they felt lost and unfulfilled. A significant number of clients wanted help to get their dream job or win a coveted promotion or improve their relationships at work or home.

THE 7C'S ARE

- Curiosity
- Creativity
- Competence
- Connection
- Communication
- Conflict (Resolution)
- Clarity

Each C plays a role in getting you closer to the life you truly want. Each C feeds into the other and leads to greater levels of conviction and confidence. Conscious awareness and practice of these will lead to insights, tools and strategies to create your abundant life.

PART 4

In subsequent chapters we will explore each C in detail. You will be invited to reflect on the things you read and put into practice what you've learnt. Once you understand and internalise its meaning, you will become aware of how it shows up in your life. That awareness will allow for a more intentional approach to how you see yourself and the world you live in.

You might identify where your strengths lie, and how you can further enhance the impact of your gifts. It will bring to life areas where you need to do a bit more work to create greater balance and harmony.

Self-knowledge and awareness of our place in the world engenders greater compassion for self, a deeper understanding of both our gifts and limitations, and forges pathways towards a more abundant life. As you begin to lead a more conscious and confident life, you will find living in the flow state becomes a natural way of being for you.

You will find some questions and points for reflection in each of the following chapters. Even if you pick just one per day, or even per week, you might discover things about yourself that change how you feel and the way you live.

Having a separate journal will help you keep notes and record any reflections and observations. On my website you can find a PDF worksheet with a summary of each C and the exercises that will help you make the most of what you've learnt.

1.

PART 4

Curiosity is defined as a desire to know or learn something. It has never been easier to quench that thirst for knowledge. Answers to every imaginable question are a mere Google search or *Hey Siri* away. It is the fast food equivalent of satisfying curiosity.

Warren Berger, author of *A More Beautiful Question*, says, *"You don't learn unless you question."* And, therefore, curiosity is the art of asking questions. He goes on to say, *"What if our schools could train students to be better lifelong learners and better adapters to change, by enabling them to be better questioners?"*

We are born curious. A newborn is thrust into a completely new environment with limited conscious knowledge of how to respond to various stimuli. A child seeks to understand this new world through their senses: watching, listening, touching, feeling and experiencing. There's not a great deal of thinking involved. In those early days and weeks children are like sponges: simply observing, absorbing, and responding without necessarily knowing how or why.

So, why is it that most children lose their natural curiosity within a few years of being at school, a place of learning where, in theory, they should be at their most inquisitive? American educator, media theorist and social critic Neil Postman once said, *"Children go into school as question marks and leave school as periods."*

In some cultures, asking questions is tantamount to dissent and disrespect. In India, where I grew up, we were taught to treat older people and those in positions of authority with respect, even reverence. Questioning their knowledge or authority was considered rude and impudent. Many other cultures in Southeast Asia are similarly suspicious of those who ask questions. Asking questions risks disturbing the status quo. It upsets the carefully balanced hierarchy. Even innocent curiosity is viewed as impertinent inquisitiveness.

In the western world, where some of these cultural dogmas don't apply to the same extent, curiosity has become a casualty of the need for speed and a quest for productivity. We live in a world that prizes fast solutions. There's no time nor patience for idle curiosity, the kind in which you ask questions without knowing if there will be an answer, and being OK with not having one. It might even be derogatively labelled as daydreaming and dawdling. *Do more, dream less* is the mantra drilled into us from an early age with the focus on doing and turning dreams into reality as quickly as possible.

Understanding Curiosity

Before you can get curious about something you have to become aware of its presence and want to know more. To become aware you must first notice or observe. To notice or observe something you have to direct your attention towards it. The more complete and undivided your attention, the more fully you become immersed in the act of observing. Where your attention goes, your energy flows. This phenomenon is called presence. Being fully present is the most fertile ground for the seeds of curiosity.

For curiosity to truly flourish, you must adopt a beginner's mindset. If you go into a situation believing you already know what to expect, you are unlikely to give it your undivided attention. In his book, *A More Beautiful Question*, Warren Berger uses the word *Vuja de* to mean seeing old familiar things as if for the very first time. It means setting aside what you know or think you know and experiencing it with a fresh perspective.

Deja Vu is the feeling you get from having already seen something before. The curiosity here may arise from wanting to know what if anything has changed since your last experience of it. Some people enjoy re-reading a book or watching a movie again and again because they want to revisit the experience and see what they missed the previous time. Or if their interpretation of what they saw the last time has stayed the same.

Extrapolation and projection are the antitheses of curiosity. You have an experience, and you use that experience as the basis to predict what will happen in the future. That is how extrapolation works. For instance, your life has a routine and a rhythm to it. As you look five years out, you are unlikely to forecast a radically different life. It is more likely to be an evolved version of what you have today. An example of projection is when we look at a situation and create a story around it that is based on our own experience of a similar situation or on how we are feeling at that particular moment in time. If you're a fearful person, even normal interactions are likely to be tinged with mistrust and cynicism.

Familiarity and extrapolation are important elements of the status quo. After years of conditioning that has made us conform and not question, the mundane familiarity of the status quo feels safer than the unpredictability of the unknown. It takes a disruptive force, such as a global pandemic, or an unexpected life event, such as a health setback, a job loss, a break up of a significant relationship, or the death of a loved one, to shake us out of our complacency.

Curiosity is about questions. The word "question" has the word "quest" in it. In its purest sense curiosity must be viewed as a quest for knowing and understanding: open ended, expansive and sometimes inconclusive. It must not be embarked on with a predetermined end in mind. Those who embark on such a quest must be willing to accept that multiple answers might be just as likely as no answers at all. It sometimes means asking uncomfortable questions and receiving unpalatable answers. It takes a highly evolved child-like mind to treat all those possibilities with equanimity. Every one of us had that kind of mind once, when we were children. With some training, we can be curious again.

Tulika

Tulika loves creating change in her life by consciously disrupting the status quo. Her motto is that life exists outside your comfort zone. If life is getting too comfortable then it is time to move on.

She and her husband both had successful careers in banking in India. When it got comfortable they uprooted and moved to Singapore. When that started to feel cosy, they upped sticks and arrived in Switzerland where they've been for a year.

"Each such move is a growth phase and isn't initially easy to adapt to. My husband is willing to take the leap with me. I embrace newness. I've started learning German to become more comfortable with the locals. I consciously choose to go into the unknown, but I also experience the difficulties this can bring. I then explore what is making me feel uncomfortable and then work on it. We send each other calendar invites a year from now. There are a hundred things I want

to do in my life. The calendar invites have to be aspirational, but in the present tense."

Tulika's openness to new experiences, people, places and opportunities is mixed with empathy, genuine interest and an absence of judgement. This is the essence of curiosity.

When I ask her how she came to embrace this unusual way of living she tells me about her nomadic childhood. She says, *"growing up, I changed schools fifteen times. I got finely attuned to what people thought of me and expected of me. So I learnt to be who I thought they thought I should be. It was very difficult to be authentic. It was exhausting to be a different face for different people. But being a nomad was where I found a sense of home."*

Such a way of life can sometimes turn people into people pleasers who will do anything in order to fit in. Tulika was blessed with a role model who helped her stay true to herself and to others. *"My grandfather was a huge influence on me. He taught me to be really honest in my engagements and actions. He urged me to not do things just to please others, to know what I really wanted. And if I was confused and not sure what I wanted, I was to tell others that I was confused. My grandfather was modern in his way of thinking – even more than my parents. I learnt from him that you start ageing when you stop learning and adapting. He read a lot. He believed that anything you don't know is just a small information gap away – and that gap can be bridged."* As an example of how he stayed relevant and was tuned into what the younger generation were doing she tells me, *"He knew all the Justin Bieber songs and the lingo young people used."*

Tulika also directs her curiosity towards herself and what's going on inside her. *"The challenge is navigating my inner world and the patterns of my childhood and examining them in an unbiased manner. I'm a very independent person. The way I deal with difficult situations is by being in my own corner, even if that means taking ten minutes to check in with myself. I learnt that I need to hold my own hand during very difficult times."* I love this. We can all learn to do this.

What I particularly admire about Tulika and her unusual approach to life is that she doesn't expect the leap of faith to always result in happiness or a better life. Embarking on an adventure with the expectation of a certain outcome is not in the true spirit of curiosity. She says, *"when we came to Basel, my husband's career took an improved trajectory. For me, it didn't feel that way. I felt I was spending a lot of my time doing household chores and caring for my child. I couldn't find 'my win' during the day. This made me unhappy and resentful. Then one day, I made a list of all the things I do. I became kind and considerate towards myself and reminded myself that diamonds are created under great pressure. This was my way of becoming a better person."*

What's your brand of Curiosity?

Curiosity comes in different guises. Our different senses and centres of intelligence provide us with different ways in which we can be curious.

You might be visually observant, or be more sensitive to sounds, or notice taste, smell or touch. You might be more alert to facts, figures and information, or you might have a strong emotional radar, or pick up the energy in a room and go by your gut instinct.

PART 4

There's one kind of curiosity that leads you to burrow your way down an intellectual rabbit hole, wherein each question leads to another related question that takes you deeper and deeper until you become an expert on that subject. People who exercise this kind of curiosity might not be satiated until they know everything there is to know about a certain topic. This might be their approach to learning – focused, intense and intentional. People who have a range of interests that they become experts in are called polymaths.

Then there's the kind of curiosity that is like a network of related strands of information. You begin with one question which leads to another question that may or may not be directly related to the original subject matter. People with this kind of curiosity are likely to dabble, flit from one topic of interest to another, picking up lessons and learning here and there, building a little nest egg of knowledge that serves a purpose. They may not be expert at anything, but their general knowledge makes them interesting, and often more useful people to be around.

The latter kind of curiosity is often disparaged in a world that prizes the expert. People often apologise for being a Jack of all trades. I'd like to defend Jack. The full saying is *"Jack of all trades is a master of none, but oftentimes is better than a master of one"*.

We need generalists as much as we need experts. After all, if you are unwell, your first port of call is to your family doctor who is a general practitioner. He or she can then direct you to the medical specialist if that was necessary. Without the help of the friendly generalist, we'd all have to self-diagnose our problems and find the relevant expert.

The six steps to exercising healthy Curiosity

1. Become fully present and observe (without seeking to change anything)
2. Frame open-ended questions (what, why, how, when)
3. Stay open minded and non-judgmental, no matter what the response or what you find
4. Pay attention to the responses using all your senses (look, listen, feel and sense)
5. Check you've understood correctly (reflect back)
6. If relevant, ask further questions to deepen your understanding

SUMMARY

Curiosity is defined as a desire to know or learn something. Warren Berger, author of *A More Beautiful Question*, says, "You don't learn unless you question." And, therefore, curiosity is the art of asking questions. All learning begins with a question.

Before you can get curious about something you have to become aware of its presence and want to know more. To become aware you must first notice or observe. To notice or observe something you have to direct your attention towards it. The more complete and undivided your attention, the more fully you become immersed in the act of observing and noticing.

Curiosity comes in different guises. Our different senses and centres of intelligence provide us with different ways in which we can be curious. We are born curious, and yet our social conditioning prioritises speed and solutions at the

PART 4

expense of curiosity. We can all learn to cultivate curiosity and become more comfortable with not knowing. First we must learn to slow down, pay attention and become truly present. This is followed by framing open ended questions, being patient and going deeper, further or on a detour into related areas of inquiry. Exploring your own brand of curiosity can be a really fun and eye-opening experience.

Get curious about what's going on with you, inside you and around you. Become a dispassionate observer of your own thoughts and feelings. Underlying every thought is a feeling, and each feeling spawns out thousands of thoughts. Every thought in turn triggers a feeling, creating a positive or negative feedback loop. The idea is to become aware, acknowledge and accept what you find without judgement. Giving the feeling a name and really noting the nuances is powerful. For instance, a feeling of melancholy is different to sadness borne out of grief. Irritation is a version of anger but manifests itself quite differently. Each feeling is a member of a broader family of emotions longing to be acknowledged for its own uniqueness and purpose.

EXERCISES

Take at least a few minutes each day to check in with yourself. In particular, do this when you notice you've been triggered into emotions that are uncomfortable and likely to be suppressed. The more often you do this, the more it becomes a habit of a lifetime.

Ask yourself these questions as you check in with yourself and notice what you observe.

1. *What is this feeling I just experienced?* This is particularly useful when you've had a thought or feeling that is intense and hard to process or even express. Identifying and labelling it is a great step towards acknowledging it.

2. *Where in my body do I notice this feeling as a sensation?* Becoming aware of the part of your body where certain feelings are generated from or stored in is very helpful. It will later help connect the dots and decipher the language of your body.

3. *If I could, how would I be expressing this feeling?* This is a great way to check if you've correctly identified the feeling. It also offers a range of possibilities for you to choose from and become more intentional in how you express uncomfortable or big feelings.

4. *What was the stimulus that triggered this feeling?* Finding connections between triggers and feelings helps us take greater control and pre-empt or prepare for events that make us feel bad.

5. *What is the story I am telling myself that is causing these feelings? Or conversely, what thoughts and stories are being generated as a result of these feelings?* This is a great way to become a conscious editor of the harmful stories you tell yourself. Reframing a thought or a story is a powerful way to tap into a more positive feeling. Looking at things from a different perspective can achieve a similar effect.

6. *When I look at myself in the mirror, who and what do I see? What thoughts and feelings do I notice in regards to what I see?* This is a powerful way to notice any self-judgement and self-criticism.

7. *What is the one thing I've never noticed before and can become curious about in my external, physical world?* This might be something familiar in your home, an item of furniture or a member of your family (!) that you take for granted and never really paid attention to. Or it might be the flowers in your neighbour's garden that you've walked past each day.

2.

Creativity is often linked with artistic endeavours, such as music, drama, painting, writing, etc. People often say, "I'm not a very creative person" as an excuse or apology for being logical or science driven. I've also heard people say, "I used to be very creative as a child but now I don't have time for it."

Left Brain vs. Right Brain

High achievers, and those with the so-called type A personality, often describe themselves as left-brained. Perhaps this is offered as an explanation for why they are ambitious and competitive. The left side of the brain is responsible for logic, problem solving and linear (sequential, repetitive and organised) ways of responding to stimuli. Science, Technology, Engineering and Maths are areas of expertise that rely on the ability to be logical, sequential and precise with limited need for emotional input. The right side of the brain is responsible for non-linear (does not follow a logical, sequential or a provable pattern) functions such as imagination, intuition and emotional intelligence.

We're born with a brain that has a left and a right side, so what those labels really mean is that we're exercising more of one side of the brain than the other. In the same way that your dominant arm is likely to be the stronger one, the side of the brain you use most is likely to dominate your life. If you were to hurt your dominant arm and it was in a cast for six weeks, your other arm would step in and get stronger.

Creativity is the antithesis of conformity. Creativity thrives in the world of imagination and possibility. Creativity is playful and not bothered too much by uncertainty. Perhaps as a child you were musical, or loved to dance, enjoyed painting or played a lot of sport. As you progressed at school, your parents may have urged you to focus on your studies rather than spend time on "extracurricular" activities. Even talented creative children are advised to have a back-up plan in case their creative or sporting endeavours don't pay the bills. You can see how the left brain gets all the attention, whilst the right brain is sidelined as less relevant to the achievement of your life goals and career prospects.

The right side of the brain is also where we process and express emotions. The suppression of that side begins early. A child begins to cry because he is tired or upset. His cries are piercing and designed to get the attention of someone who will take care of him. A loving, nurturing adult picks up the child and comforts him until he is calmer. Now, imagine you are that nurturing adult and this happens in a shopping mall, or on public transport full of other people. Suddenly, the child's shrill cries invade the ambience of that closed space. Unless you can calm the child down fairly quickly, people start looking at you, judging you, berating you under their breath for bringing a noisy child into a crowded space. Sensing this growing antagonism you become more focused on shushing the distraught child. "Now, that's enough. Come on, there's no need to cry. Here, let me stick this soother into your mouth to shut you up." After a few such experiences, the child receives the message – it is not OK to cry in public. And oh, it is probably best not to cry at all because it is not received well by others.

The same goes for certain positive emotions. Notice how you respond when someone is "too happy" or laughing out loud in a way that is not inclusive of everyone else. Girls, in particular, grow up being told it is unladylike to show too much of a positive emotion, because it may draw unwelcome attention from the wrong kind of people. And thus begins the suppression of spontaneous, unadulterated desire, joy and laughter.

The logical left brain is now in full control. And it will repeatedly bring your attention to the fact that letting it be in control is better for you. You will be more qualified, you will know things that other people will respect and value you for, and you will improve your chances of finding a career that pays well and has potential for growth. It will also invite you to look at how many poverty-stricken creatives there are in the world, and how much riskier it is to gamble your life in the hope that you might become the next Tom Cruise or Taylor Swift.

For many, the Covid-19 pandemic was the disruptive force that shook them out of their white-collar, logical, analytical, financially motivated status quo. People were forced into lockdown and no longer had their usual left brain driven routines. Some of them turned to creative pursuits as a way to channel their pent-up energy and feelings of isolation. Many small businesses sprung up from kitchens and bedrooms. People took art lessons. Some wrote poetry. Others turned to music. The right side of the brain was finally allowed to get into the driving seat, even if only until "normal life" resumed. And for many of these brave individuals, the taste of this different way of living made the post-Covid new normal a more balanced one.

If you are not one of those people, do not despair. Thank your left brain for the responsibility it takes on and fulfils non-stop every waking hour of the day. It has kept you safe, allowed you to get where you are in your life, given you the language to communicate with others, to make rational sense of the information that bombards you every second of your life.

Priya

My cousin Priya's life was turned upside down when after eleven years of being in remission her cancer returned, and this time it was terminal. Priya was a post doctoral fellow in Virology who could not imagine a life in which she was not a scientist. Until recently she was on the frontline of genetic research seeking treatments for complex health conditions. Her health setback pressed pause on her career as she underwent treatment. At first this caused Priya a great deal of anguish as the days seem to stretch before her without professional purpose. As the treatment progressed, she decided to spend her days doing things she never previously had time for. After her first cancer diagnosis Priya took up photography, solo travel and writing poetry. In 2019, she published her book of poems titled *a book of one and a half choices*. She continued to express her innermost feelings through poetry and took up singing lessons. Priya had a sweet lilting voice. As a consequence of the tumour and the damage it caused to parts of her brain, Priya began to lose the ability to connect thoughts with language: a condition called Aphasia. But she was still able to sing. When it became harder to express herself with words, Priya took up painting. Her art took all who knew her by surprise as it was not something she had previously shown an inclination for. She recently produced a beautiful work of art with her left hand (she is right-handed) after she suffered a partial paralysis on the right side of her body. Priya's paintings with the vivid colours and eloquent strokes became the language with which she expressed herself. It was as if the right side of her brain stepped in while the left side was out of action. She bore her troubles with dignity and a smile, with creativity and courage, inspiring all whose lives she touched.

I invite you to explore ways for your right brain to get involved. You don't even have to take up art, music or dance, although they're all fantastic ways to get out of the rut of a repetitive, left-brain driven life. Give it a chance to play, to create meaning and to be in control, at least some of the time. Allow yourself to feel, to fly, to flow. Read on to find ways that you can do this without making seismic shifts in your life.

Creativity at work

People often make the mistake of giving up their day job to follow their "creative passion". The hard graft of making your craft pay its way involves things you may be ill-prepared for. This includes self-promotion, setting the "right price" and dealing with criticism and rejection. If you're a talented writer or musician, what you really want to be doing is writing or playing music. All the other things may be out of your comfort zone and can feel soul destroying. *Why burden the free spirit of your creativity by expecting it to pay your bills?*

When you nurture your creativity and let it flow towards where it needs to go, amazing things happen. For years Elizabeth Gilbert, best-selling author of *Big Magic* and *Eat Pray Love*, had a day job unrelated to her writing. She had been a published writer of short stories and had three books to her name before she felt ready to turn it into a vocation. It was only after the runaway success of *Eat Pray Love* that she gave up her day job.

In her book *Big Magic* she talks about how as a young sixteen-year-old she made a promise to her creativity, that she would always take care of it and never expect it to take care of her material needs. Of course there was a goal: to become a successful published author. There was commitment to put in the hard work that this endeavour demanded. There was courage to write even if no one read it. But there was no agenda or ultimatum. She didn't say, if in the next two years I don't make enough money from my writing so I can quit my day job, then I will take it as a message from the universe that I am not meant to be a writer!

The universe sends us no such messages. Creativity is a gift that every one of us has. If you have imagination, you are creative. The universe is a benign force that wants us to succeed. It wants us to go boldly forth and really make the most of this amazing opportunity to experience life as a human. It wants us to get clear on what we want and what we need. And it wants us to ask for those things clearly and with complete conviction.

Elizabeth Gilbert accepted her gift of creativity with gratitude and grace. She lovingly, respectfully gave it permission to be, to grow and to flow. She did not burden it with expectations that it would support her, pay her bills or earn her external validation. She nourished it. She worked hard for it and with it. She invested in it. And over time, it reaped rewards far beyond what she could have ever imagined.

PART 4

What is Creativity?

Creativity is the ability to create something that did not previously exist. It might be a product or an idea or a novel solution to a problem. It can also be an energy or an experience.

Creativity thrives in the land of possibility. Open your eyes, ears and other senses, and follow your curiosity.

Creativity can be driven by a need or a want. It is fuelled with imagination, resourcefulness and skill.

Creativity is thinking outside the box. The "box" is a set of rules and procedures that define the status quo. Most inventions were as a result of such creative thinking.

Here are some everyday examples of creativity that show that we are all more creative than we think we are.

You are creative if you:

- *Use your imagination to conjure up new possibilities and innovative solutions to problems.*
- *Enjoy reusing, repairing and rejuvenating old things, giving them a new lease of life.*
- *Love DIY and often find ways to fix things by using your common sense.*
- *Made the customer engagement process at work more fun, leading to an increase in sales and better feedback.*
- *Cook with whatever ingredients you can find in your refrigerator to create a delicious new recipe.*
- *Enjoy gardening and the process of designing, planning and planting.*

- *Declutter, clean and decorate your living space to make it warm and welcoming.*
- *Write or paint or play a musical instrument just because it makes you happy.*

WHAT'S YOUR BRAND OF CREATIVITY?

Outcome driven

If you're a goal-driven creative, you are a problem solver who uses your curiosity, imagination and resourcefulness to achieve a clearly defined outcome. The free flow of creativity is tempered with a loose structure in the form of the end goal, a time frame and available resources. The possibilities are more in the realm of the "how to" rather than the "what it can be".

An example of such a creative pursuit might be found in the profession of an architect, or a software programmer, or a website designer, or even a seamstress. The client who has commissioned the work might not always know in precise terms what they want, but they will usually know what they want that end product to do for them.

The first step is to be curious. Ask lots of questions and really understand the problem the customer is seeking to solve. Alternatively, there might not be a problem as such, but rather the desire for something different or new. In that case, getting as clear a picture of what they are seeking to achieve is the first step towards creating the desired outcome.

This is a great skill, because most people don't know exactly what they want. Helping someone get clear on what they want, being able to connect with someone else's vision when they don't have the language to describe it to you, is a skill that requires both sides of the brain to engage. There are many professions that draw on this kind of creativity which proves that you can make a living from being creative.

Inspiration driven

An alternative way to live a creative life is to cultivate opportunities for inspiration to touch you. Some of my most creative inspirations have come to me when I was washing up or taking a shower or walking with headphones playing my favourite music playlist. Allowing your mind to wander freely, or simply be still and fully present, are fertile ground for new ideas.

Every creative process begins with an idea. It might be an "Aha!" moment that offers a glimpse of a solution to a niggling problem. Or it can be a seed of possibility that becomes planted in your mind.

In her book *Big Magic*, Elizabeth Gilbert explores the concept of our world being populated with not just living things and inanimate objects, but also with ideas. She describes ideas as if they are little invisible butterflies flitting about, hoping someone will notice them, adopt them and bring them to life. As if driven by a survival instinct, the idea will keep searching for the person who will give them form and substance. It doesn't understand the notion of exclusivity. Two people who have never met, never interacted in any way and never been exposed to one another's thoughts and activities might create almost identical solutions to a universal problem.

An oak tree produces millions of seeds in its lifetime, but only a handful of these grow into mature oaks. It is the same with ideas. Not every idea is a good one. Not every idea shows up at the right time. Not all ideas are meant to be brought to fruition. Some ideas are tricksters and lead on to a dead-end. Not every idea needs to be an acorn with decades before it turns into a mature oak. Some ideas are short-lived and show up to fulfil a need. All ideas need a carrier, a nurturer and an executor (not the legal or axe wielding kind).

SUMMARY

Creativity is often linked with artistic endeavours, such as music, drama, painting, writing, etc. People often say, "I'm not a very creative person" as an excuse or apology for being logical or science driven. I've also heard people say, "I used to be very creative as a child but now I don't have time for it."

Creativity is the antithesis of conformity. Creativity is the ability to create something that did not previously exist, driven by a need or a want. Creativity thrives in the world of imagination and possibility. Creativity is thinking outside the box. Creativity is playful and not bothered too much by uncertainty.

High achievers, and those with the so-called type A personality, often describe themselves as left-brained. The left side of the brain is responsible for logic, problem solving and linear (sequential, repetitive and organised) ways of responding to stimuli. The right side of the brain is responsible for non-linear (does not follow a logical, sequential or a provable pattern) functions such as imagination, intuition and emotional intelligence. We're born with a brain that has a left and a right side, so what those labels really mean is that we are exercising more of one side of the brain than the other.

Creativity can be inspiration driven or outcome driven. Getting creative is a lovely way of bringing a greater balance to how we use our brain. By giving your dominant side of the brain permission to routinely take a break and temporarily step back from its role of being the primary provider of mental capacity in your life, you give it a chance to rest, recharge and become rejuvenated. The underutilised right side of the brain finally gets a chance to be in charge and prove to you that it too has a purpose and powers. The most important of which is that it allows you to go below the surface level of your thoughts and connect more deeply with your own and other people's feelings. Creative expression through art or music or dance or even sport are powerful ways for the mind and body to become more deeply connected. Commit to trying at least one of the suggested exercises each day so you can build your creative muscle.

EXERCISES

Here are a few things you can do:

1. Give your imagination permission to roam at least once a day. Take a topic, any topic, and set your mind free and see what happens.
2. Think back to your childhood. What creative pursuits did you have? Could you pick up one of them and do it just for fun?
3. Pick a task you routinely perform – such as driving to work, or cooking dinner or brushing your teeth. Deliberately choose a different route, try a different recipe or use your non-dominant arm to complete the task. Get yourself out of autopilot mode.
4. Let's say you're looking for answers to a problem or challenge. Instead of going with the obvious solution, first make a list of all the possible solutions, even if they seem highly improbable.
5. Listen to a podcast or watch a film or read about someone whom you know nothing or have previously not taken an interest in. Can you find just one thing about them that you like, admire or resonate with?
6. Join a group or community of creative people – this can be online, but better still in person. When we are with creative people, their energy and creative spirit can rub off on us.

PART 4

7. Say yes to something entirely on the back of your intuition. And then go with the flow. Notice what happens: how you feel and what you do. Notice any changes in your behaviour.

3.

PART 4

In our modern world, competence has become synonymous with qualifications. Labels and letters that "prove" that you have a talent or intellect, that you've done the work needed to acquire a skill or an expertise.

You may have spent years and possibly a lot of money to acquire these qualifications. Now you rightly expect to reap the rewards of this investment of your time and money. And thus begins the rat race: the forward march to stay ahead of the pack with a better job, more pay and greater social recognition. Anything less and you feel like a failure.

Competence is defined as the ability to do something successfully or efficiently. Humans have been able to do this long before there was formal education that resulted in grades and qualifications.

This obsession with external recognition and validation has resulted in the unfortunate habit of overlooking things we know and do well that have no labels or fancy letters. These are things we do every day, often without conscious thought or intent, that make life better for ourselves and others.

Our march towards varying levels of competency begins from an early age. Learning to walk. Learning to communicate – read, write, speak and listen. Learning to comprehend, comply and create meaning. And so much more.

There is a reason why our early education tends to be prescriptive and structured. We are taught to conform and be disciplined. We wear a school uniform. We follow a strict timetable. And we are evaluated on how well we remember what we've been taught. Years later we may forget most of what we learnt, but crucially we will have developed a core competency which will become the foundation of all future learning. Strong foundations create greater possibilities. With possibilities come choices.

When I was growing up in India, there were fewer options and one might say life was simpler as a result. Your exam results and your aptitude for certain subjects determined your future. If you were a bright student with excellent grades, you were expected to do medicine or engineering (i.e. science and maths-based subjects). If your academic achievements were less stellar, you might go on to study business or accounting. And if you were one of those dreamers whose grades didn't quite match your imagination, you'd do a degree in arts or go into an area of work that was paid poorly even if it created immeasurable value to society – such as teaching or care in the community. The lowest paid continue to be manual workers without whom life as we know it would grind to a halt.

Ironically, the brightest students in India who graduate from some of India's top engineering colleges go on to do an MBA and then work in finance, marketing or consulting. The engineering degree is a foot in the door to a career that is unlikely to ever need their specialist knowledge. This might seem like a waste of four years of top class education, and unfair to candidates with different (lesser) qualifications more suited for the role of a graduate trainee.

I have met with many such engineers turned MBAs turned corporate executives. I went to business school with them. They know they are part of an academic elite in the top 1% of the country, that they have overcome a great many challenges along the way, and that if all else fails, they have a world-class qualification to fall back on. They have sharp minds and have worked unbelievably hard to get to where they are. They work well under the pressure and have been academically successful in the face of intense competition.

A top recruiter is paying for this self-belief and competitive spirit. Compared to what they have learnt, the work they will be expected to do is unlikely to be as intellectually challenging. It may demand a series of professional qualifications and skills that they will have to acquire on the job – such as selling, dealing with difficult clients or suppliers, and working as a team rather than as an individual contributor.

The recruiter is buying into the expectation that these confident recruits can be nurtured to become part of the future corporate leadership. It is also a status symbol for an organisation to be attractive to the crème de la crème. The race to be the best begins here too – it is an expensive one that shuts out people who may be more suited for the job, likely to be more loyal and cost significantly less than these overqualified candidates. It further fosters a sense of inequality that divides the privileged elite from the rest of the population.

The value of qualifications

Most qualifications have a shelf life. Unless learning is put into practice, over time it diminishes in value. Imagine if you passed your driving test and then didn't drive for the next five years. Or if you graduated from medical school but never actually worked as a doctor on real patients. This is why recruiters look for relevant work experience when considering suitability for a job, unless they plan to train you and are more interested in your aptitude than your experience.

Competence isn't just about what you know, it is about what you do with what you know. It is also about what you can do when you don't know – i.e. how able and willing are you to deal with things that are unknown and unforeseeable. In the real world, competence is about resourcefulness. It is about resilience. It is about getting a job done.

If you were to do a detailed audit of the things you do for yourself and for others, how many of those skills were learnt at school or through your higher education? You might be surprised to find that you are making a difference to people's lives in ways you never realised or ever considered important. And you may discover skills and competencies that hold keys to finding greater fulfilment in ways you never thought possible.

Aadhya

Aadhya grew up with a natural flair for competition that was fuelled by a burning desire to excel and be the best. Even coming second felt like failure and elicited the disapproval of her parents. Aside from being an accomplished student, Aadhya was successful at sports. At one time, over a space of eighteen months she represented her State in seven different sports. She enjoyed being a leader and taking charge. From an early age she understood the importance of portraying the right image if she was to be respected as a leader.

She says, *"It all began with wanting to project a certain self-image. At 11, I became a team captain in sports and other fields at school. I had to lead people who were older than me and it was important that they accept me. I needed to understand the people in my team, what made them tick*

PART 4

and how, as their leader, I could help them deliver their best whilst also making me look my best. I would observe myself and, at the end of each day, I would spend time reflecting on what I did, why I did it, how it impacted others and their lives. What did it say about me? What did the other person take away? It started at a basic level, now it has become a more complex internal dialogue that has become a lifelong end of day habit."

This quest for perfection meant that each day she *Kaizened* (the Japanese term for continuous improvement) her way into constantly trying to improve herself. It was also a systematic way to eliminate mistakes and maximise the chances of success.

The underlying emotion that drove this behaviour from an early age was fear: in particular, fear of failure, which she says did not leave her until she was in her thirties. As a child, she dealt with her fear with more fear, and by making sure she did not make the same mistake again. The turning point for Aadhya was the birth of her child. *"After I had a child, that desire to be the best became more tempered, even though I am still very competitive. Where I am in my life now, I have a much bigger fear of not being around for my child. Now, in my professional field, I have no fear, but in my personal life I live with extreme fear. I am more conscious of my health."*

When fear is a core emotion, the person will often rely on the rational mind via the brain as their main centre of intelligence. Facts and figures provide certainty. Logic trumps over supposition. They are less likely to be driven by their heart or gut. Gathering more information, constant vigilance and becoming the most competent person in the room become go-to strategies to ensure safety. This can lead to overthinking, mental stress and a desire to eliminate mistakes.

Aadhya says, *"my perfectionism feeds into and feeds off overthinking. Professionally, it would keep me on the edge. Everyone became a competitor. I'm still very competitive, but I have let go of the hypercompetitive baggage of being the best at everything. I have realised that the parameters of competition can be manyfold, and not always from a single perspective. For instance, one person's strength could be speed, whereas someone else's might be endurance. As an individual, learning humility has been life changing for me, and it is as a consequence of having my daughter."*

Aadhya is very self-aware, and it has been a lifelong quest for her to get to know herself better. She became fascinated by the concept of the Johari window – a framework for self-awareness. (We talk about this in more detail later in this chapter.) Her focus is projected outwards towards understanding how others see her, and in particular getting to know aspects of herself that she doesn't know but others do. She realises that people often see her differently to her intention. This can lead to cognitive dissonance and get in the way of achieving the outcomes in the best possible way.

Aadhya recalls a time in her professional life that brought home the importance of emotional intelligence alongside professional brilliance. She says, *"Ten years ago, a mentor pointed out to me that my peers saw me as a threat because I was articulate and fearless. In meetings with senior management, I would say the right things which put me in the spotlight. My team and my bosses loved me. She urged me to find a way to make friends with these peers so they too would like me. For someone who was always focused on the goal, this was a very interesting challenge. So I had to change my persona to someone who was there to listen. That listening helped me understand why they were doing what they were doing and why they were not helping with something. The reasons were not always professional. That persona opened my eyes to a new way of being and (in due course) became an authentic part of me. It was tough because I like to take charge and get things done, but it doesn't always sit well with others. Motherhood changed me and my bigger goals."*

Aadhya's experience shows us that we all have the ability to evolve and reinvent ourselves. This is an important lesson: our persona may feel like a mask that is quite separate from who we are deep down. But if the mask fits and feels right, there is no reason why it can't become who we are. Being authentic doesn't mean never changing. You could fake it until you make it. This is true both in our personal lives and in the professional arena.

When it comes to new opportunities, you don't have to wait until you have everything you believe is required of you. Every cell in your body is ready, willing and able to learn, to regenerate and start anew. You are more ready than you think you are.

THE FOUR STAGES OF COMPETENCE

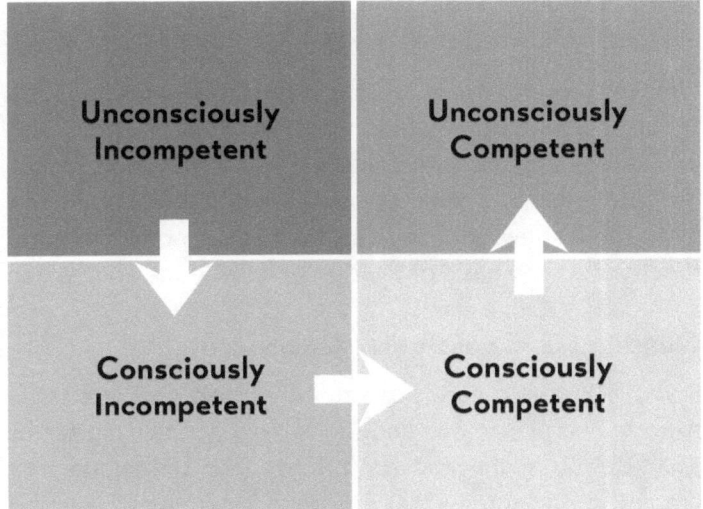

The psychological concept of the four stages of competence was later developed into the basis of a "learning ladder" by Noel Burch at Gordon Training International.

Quadrant 1: Unconsciously Incompetent

It is true that you only know what you know, which means there is a vast labyrinth of potential knowledge that you are (and might always be) unaware of. This is the first quadrant on the top left: *you don't know that you don't know*, or in other words, you are blissfully ignorant.

Quadrant 2: Consciously Incompetent

Then something happens and you *become aware of your ignorance*. Maybe an event occurs that creates a need that did not previously exist. You realise you're missing something. At this point, you might either become curious and want to know more or you might consider it unworthy of your attention and therefore choose not to bother pursuing that line of inquiry.

It makes sense to focus on your strengths and preferences. After all, you might live and work with others with whom you have a symbiotic relationship. This allows you to focus on certain things while they take care of the rest. We don't all have to know and do everything. Our modern society functions on the basis of division of knowledge and labour.

Quadrant 3: Consciously Competent

If you follow your curiosity, you might take concrete steps towards learning more about this new subject matter or skill set. You might read about it, or enrol on a course, or embark on a journey that offers an experiential learning opportunity. During this stage you are consciously working towards becoming more knowledgeable and competent.

Quadrant 4: Unconsciously Competent

The last quadrant is where the knowledge and the skill has become so ingrained in you that you don't know you have it, or that you are doing it, or even how you are doing it. To an outside observer, it might seem effortless. In reality, it is the result of many hours of conscious effort that has now become an extension of who you are. Alternatively, it could be something we've always had and never realised its value or that not everyone has it. There is a potential goldmine of things we don't know we know.

The second and third quadrants are where we can exercise judgement and discernment. Once we know ourselves well, once we have clarity of intent and purpose, we can become intentional about raising our levels of conscious competence.

When we repeatedly put our conscious learning into practice, doing it better each time, adding refinements and perfecting our craft, it can become an integral part of us. At this stage, we no longer really have to think about it or indeed consciously recall how we do things. This is when we are deemed to be unconsciously competent. This is the flow-state where knowing, being and doing all blend into one another.

DIFFERENT LEARNING STYLES: THE VARK MODEL

Life provides us with plenty of opportunities for learning. Once we've left the formal and prescriptive education system, there are many more opportunities to choose what we learn, how we learn it and what we do with what we learn. The internet and the many digital platforms of learning are a gift for anyone who loves to learn.

In 1992 Neil Fleming and Colleen Mills devised a way students could understand their learning preferences better so that their education could be tailored in ways that helped them learn best. They postulated that, broadly speaking, there were four learning styles.

Visual – through visualisation and where the information is presented in the form of pictures, charts, diagrams, flow charts and other visual cues.

Aural/Auditory – through heard or spoken words, listening to lectures, podcasts, audiobooks and talking through the information or problem with oneself out loud or with another person.

Read/Write – through text-based input and output, where information is presented as words in books, essays, manuals, presentations, articles etc.

Kinaesthetic – through experiencing things via practice, simulation and case studies. The focus is on its connection with reality so the concepts feel tangible and can be grasped, held, tasted or felt.

Do you know what your preferred learning style is? When I was growing up in India, the Read/Write style was the only way for us to learn, and how well we did relied on our capacity to remember and regurgitate information verbatim in our exams. It is my least favourite way to learn. I find the other three styles suit me much better, and if I had my time at school again and had the opportunity to learn a different way, I might learn so much more.

How well do you know yourself?

In our quest to learn how to be, act and survive in the world, our attention is generally focused outward where we perceive opportunities and danger. We might assume that because we've known ourselves all our lives, and we are inseparable from ourselves, we must obviously know ourselves better than anyone else.

Like the four stages of competence, this is a useful framework for understanding your relationship with yourself and others better.

JOHARI WINDOW

	Known to self	Not known to self
Known to others	Arena	Blind Spot
Not known to others	Façade	Unknown

The Johari Window is the brainchild of psychologists Joseph Luft and Harrington Ingham, who in 1955 created it for use in self-help groups and corporate settings. In 1990, Charles Handy renamed it The Johari House with Four Rooms. I like that better and will henceforth refer to them as rooms.

In a heuristic exercise, one aimed at helping someone learn things about themselves, a person picks a number of adjectives from a given list. These are based on words they think best describe their personality. People who know the person are also asked to pick out the same number of adjectives. These are then inserted into the grid with four rooms painting a picture of how someone sees themselves and how others see them.

Arena – This is your conscious self who is known to you and is known to others.

Façade – This is your version of who you are (or who you think you are) that is unknown or unrecognised by others.

Blind Spot – This is how others see you, but you don't recognise that version of yourself.

Unknown – The version of you that you are not consciously aware of, and neither are others.

Although there is a geometric simplicity to a framework that shows four equally sized rooms, in reality the size varies depending on the individual. A What You See Is What You Get (WYSIWYG) open-book sort of person will spend a lot more time in the Arena. A more private person would be very sparing with how much of themselves they allow others to see. They may even present a mask that is not authentic to who they really are. These two rooms suggest a great deal more conscious awareness, and we spend the majority of our lives in one of these two rooms.

Most of us struggle to see ourselves as the world sees us, and this can be the reason why our interactions and relationships don't go the way we want them to. As you go on your journey of self-discovery, you will find aspects of your personality that have lain dormant or unseen by your own eyes. The rooms named Blind Spot and Unknown are where you must dare to go if you are to become more aware of the aspects of your character and personality you do not see and may not know exist. It is where you must go to discover who you really are and what is possible for you.

SUMMARY

In our modern world, competence has become synonymous with qualifications. Labels and letters that "prove" that you have a talent or intellect, that you've done the work needed to acquire a skill or an expertise.

Competence is defined as the ability to do something successfully or efficiently. Humans have been able to do this long before there was formal education that resulted in grades and widely recognised qualifications.

Competence isn't just about what you know, it is about what you do with what you know. It is also about what you can do when you don't know – i.e. how able and willing are you to deal with things that are unknown and unforeseeable. In the real world, competence is about resourcefulness. It is about resilience. It is about getting a job done.

The psychological concept of four stages of competence helps us become aware of what we know or don't know based on whether or not we are conscious of it. The four quadrants are unconscious incompetence, conscious incompetence, conscious competence and unconscious competence. The second and third quadrants are where we can exercise judgement and discernment. Once we know ourselves well, once we have clarity of intent and purpose, we can become intentional about raising our levels of conscious competence.

There are four key learning styles – visual, auditory, text based and experiential. Becoming aware of our preferred learning style can really help us learn faster and more effectively.

PART 4

The area of learning that is paid the least amount of attention in our education system is the one where we get to know ourselves. The Johari Window or the Johari House with Four Rooms is a framework that helps us see ourselves through our conscious awareness (Arena), how others see us as we intend them to (Façade) and in ways that we are not aware of (Blindspot), and the version of ourselves that is unknown to both us and others (Unknown).

Most of us struggle to see ourselves as the world sees us, and this can be the reason why our interactions and relationships don't go the way we want them to. The rooms named Blind Spot and Unknown are where you must dare to go if you are to become more aware of the aspects of your character and personality you do not see and may not know exist. It is where you must go to discover who you really are and what is possible for you.

EXERCISES

Each day, take a moment to reflect on one of the following:

1. What did I do well today? How did it help me and/or someone else?
2. What did I learn today that I did not previously know? How will this new knowledge impact my life?
3. What gap in my knowledge did I discover today that if I filled would enhance my life? What action do I need to take in order to fill this gap?
4. What kind of impression did I leave on the people I interacted with today? Is there anything I could do differently next time?
5. What can I learn today that will make me happy, feel more secure or be at peace?
6. What can I learn today that will add value to the people in my inner circle and outer circle?
7. What am I drawn towards learning purely through following my curiosity? How will it impact my life?

4.

Connection is such an ubiquitous word and, despite its fairly obvious meaning, it can mean different things to different people and in different contexts.

As humans we make connections with our senses and our centres of intelligence – the brain, the heart and the gut. We might use logic and prior knowledge to make sense of disparate pieces of information. We might make an emotional connection to a thing, a place, an idea or a person. And we might energetically sense if something feels right or safe or attractive for us.

Most often, the connection happens without us even noticing or analysing. Let's say you walk into a room full of strangers. Depending on how comfortable you are with the unknown and being around strangers, your senses are on alert to pick up cues on whether you belong there, whether it is safe for you to be there. Your mind connects the dots and creates a picture that tells you how to respond. If you feel safe, you might stay – if not, you might take another action. If you feel welcome, you might feel yourself lighten up and relax. If you spot someone you know and like, or you make an energetic and emotional connection with that person, you feel a step closer to communicating.

So much of how we connect with our external environment happens on autopilot, beneath the awareness of our conscious mind. We give out and receive signals that shape our interactions with the world around us. To give an example, your facial expression and body language is sending out a certain vibe that you may not be aware of. How that is received by others will depend on their own life experiences and the picture they've created in their minds when connecting the dots presented by your demeanour. This is your blind spot. You might not know how others see you.

PART 4

Connecting with yourself

"Being able to feel safe with other people is probably the single most important aspect of mental health; safe connections are fundamental to meaningful and satisfying lives."

— BESSEL VAN DER KOLK

In our early years, we learn how to connect with ourselves based on how others, particularly our important others, connect with us. How the people who are supposed to love us and care for us treat us becomes a template for how we treat ourselves in later life.

It can be particularly hard if a child has grown up in an environment where the adults around them are emotionally unavailable. Perhaps the parents are too wrapped up in their own dramas to pay attention to the child's needs and wants. There is no abuse or malice or deliberate neglect, rather a benign indifference to the child's existence. The subliminal message the child might take away is that their needs and wants are not important, that they don't matter.

There are very few people who can truthfully say they had a "perfect" childhood. There is no such thing as a perfect family. Every family has a dysfunctional aspect to it. But even when there is awareness of just how far from perfect their childhood was, there is a reluctance to place blame or say anything negative about parents. Such attribution is shrouded with guilt. It feels too disrespectful. There's a fear that, like Pandora's box, once opened it can never again be shut, with all its grim consequences. After all, we don't choose our families, and there's an unwritten obligation and responsibility we may feel towards our parents in particular.

Our backpack is full of suppressed, even repressed, memories from childhood. Learning to honour these and the feelings that resulted from them is such an important aspect of connecting deeply with who we really are. We can do this without playing the blame game. Our parents were shaped by their own upbringing that may have been far more difficult than the one we experienced. Every generation is trying to do the right thing, occasionally by overcompensating for that which was denied them. But you can't be something you are not, and you can't know what you need to be if you've never yourself experienced it.

As a child, even small things can feel traumatic. Events such as being separated from your parent in a busy shopping centre, even if only for five minutes, being shouted at by a teacher in front of the whole class, being banished from your friendship group, being told you are selfish for having perfectly reasonable needs and wants, are all examples of childhood trauma.

Suppressing unpleasant memories and emotions is our body's way of keeping us safe. We may even learn strategies and coping mechanisms to avoid further trauma or minimise its impact on us. But this does not prepare us for an uncertain world that may yet be cruel to us. At a subconscious level we may repeat patterns that spiral us back into harm's way, inviting rather than averting further trauma. Or it may cause us to behave towards ourselves and others in ways that diminish our chances of living a happy and healthy life.

PART 4

Once we've made peace with the child we once were, it becomes easier to accept and forgive others who have let us down. How we connect with ourselves also impacts how we relate to others. How do you connect with yourself? You are the one person who has known you all your life and will be with you until the day you die. What would it feel like to connect with yourself so deeply that you feel seen, heard and understood by the most important person in your life: you?

Becoming an observer

Bessel Van der Kolk, in his book, *The Body Keeps the Score*, talks about the benefits of yoga in healing trauma. Both yoga and therapy use the phrases "notice that" followed by "what happens next?" He says, "Once you start approaching your body with curiosity, not fear, it allows the individual to work with their own body, mind and spirit, allowing themselves to be led from within."

In previous chapters we explored the benefits of getting curious about what's going on inside us, how we see ourselves and how the world sees us. You can do this as an objective observer who simply notices and allows aspects of your inner world to reveal itself. It's like observing yourself from the other side of a one-way mirror, like they do in police stations and research laboratories. In this kind of observation, those who are being observed don't know they are being observed. Their behaviour is not influenced by the awareness of your presence. This can be powerful and informative in an objective, non-interfering way.

Now imagine, you've asked for permission to enter the room and sit with yourself. You are no longer a dispassionate observer. You are now a compassionate witness, mirroring back to yourself what you notice, choosing your words and non-verbal cues with care. Your aim is to create a space that is non-judgmental and safe. The desired outcome is for your inner self to feel seen, heard and understood in ways that it has craved for but never before experienced.

The beauty of this approach is that it can be done at any time, any place where you feel able to be in calm solitude, and as often as you need. Connecting with yourself compassionately will involve being resolute with parts of yourself that have been unwitting saboteurs of your self-esteem. Your inner critic, for instance, might show up in unwelcome ways. Thank them for the role they've played in keeping you safe. Ask them firmly to step aside while you take care of the little child you once were, and who still lives inside you, who needs a loving, nurturing adult to keep them safe. Now you get to be the responsible, compassionate adult to your inner child.

Nivedita

Nivedita's journey of self-discovery began ten years ago. She was going through a low patch, both professionally and in terms of her health. She says, *"the first few years of the journey was finding a better way to live, becoming more aware of my surroundings. I started yoga and spent more time in nature. I remember a day in 2012 when, for the very first time, I noticed the blossoms of spring in my local park. I had lived right by this park since the mid-nineties but had never really 'seen it'. I suddenly viewed my outer world with new eyes in a way that expanded my being in a very powerful way."*

PART 4

Having experienced the wonder of really "seeing" the world she lived in, as if for the very first time, she *"turned that gaze inward, noticed things that have always been there and expressed gratitude."* She adds, *"I started counting my blessings rather than focusing on things I didn't have. I learnt to see things from multiple perspectives. I'm now much better at observing myself and noticing what's going on. Whether I'm happy, suffering, detached or emotionally attached. However, I will never fully know myself because I am always changing."*

Nivedita grew up in a small town in India within a close-knit community where the men all worked in the same factory. Gender and social class were big influences in how people behaved and interacted. She adds, *"there was a clear pecking order based on their status at work. For us kids too, our dad's position in that pecking order affected how we were perceived. The gender issue mainly related to how much marrying a daughter off would cost the parents. I wanted to relieve my parents of that burden and fought back against this norm. I was driven by a deep desire to prove myself to my parents and to others."*

Nivedita left the confines of the small community to pursue a path to greater freedom and autonomy. She chose to study engineering and create a life that was very different to the one she grew up in. *"There was sexism in the education system too, and the gender stereotyping was very clear. I was determined to pursue an area of education that I would enjoy. I wanted to be clear about my own long-term plan and choices, which included my choice in a life partner who was right for me."*

Early on in her career in banking, Nivedita and her husband moved to the UK. Moving to a different ecosystem brought its own challenges. *"The cultural differences I faced when I moved from India to the UK took a toll on my ability to build connections."* Digging deep into her pot of self-belief and competence helped her grow in confidence in the workplace. In later years, as she took the time to connect more deeply with herself, she also allowed curiosity and compassion to blossom. She adds, *"That has helped me shed some of my armour. I have always had a fear of being judged. I role-modelled stoicism and fought against machismo. In that scenario, there wasn't much room for vulnerability."*

The negative emotions Nivedita experiences most frequently are helplessness and despair. She describes it as, *"A feeling of being trapped and not being able to do anything about it. Now when this happens, the first thing I do is give it time. I let myself be. I stay quiet, withdraw, cry and stay down. I don't force myself to engage or talk. My rational brain still rules. I start to decode the entrapment and assess what options I'm missing. I accept the things I can't change. I very rarely lash out, but I make sure I can withdraw from the situation with as much grace as possible. Learning how to localise the pain (or problem) and determine the root cause of it has been a very helpful strategy."*

This is a great way to create a space between a triggering stimulus and our response. It gives us the time to acknowledge and accept what has happened and how it has made us feel. The next step is to allow these feelings to be processed and expressed in healthy ways. Nivedita admits that she is a work-in-progress. She says, *"my greatest challenge is when I find I become too much of an observer. There are not many situations in which I surprise myself. I need to do more, be me, observe less."*

Knowing yourself, why you are the way you are and how certain events make you feel is such an important step towards freedom. What you do with that knowledge and how you interact with the outside world is equally important. How we connect with others without losing ourselves in the process is key to living an abundant life.

Connecting with others

As young children, unfiltered connections came naturally to us. Children are very good at reading non-verbal cues and sensing their environment. Notice how babies respond very differently to different people. A baby might cry and be anxious when in the arms of a stressed parent. The same baby might quieten down and fall asleep in the presence of a stranger with a calm manner and soothing voice.

Social conditioning and life experiences make us wary and selective in our interactions. You may have grown up with the warning, "Stranger Danger!", which stayed with you even into adulthood. Think of all the opportunities to connect with interesting people that were lost because of a childhood conditioning intended to protect the younger, more vulnerable, you.

A stranger is simply a person you don't yet know. One of them could one day become a best friend, a life partner, a mentor or teacher or a guardian angel in your time of need. By never allowing natural connections to occur, you are closing off pathways to relationships that could change your life in ways you can't imagine.

Of course, not every connection will be right for you, and some people might create havoc and cause you pain. You can learn to read the signs and discern a "good" from a "bad" one, a healthy relationship from a damaging one. This kind of discernment is easier when you really know yourself, what works for you, what you need and want, and what your core values are. We will explore this in greater detail later in this book.

Nehaarikaa

Nehaarikaa grew up with middle-class values of hard work, honesty, and trustworthiness. She gets the big picture and uses it to figure out why we do what we do. The untimely demise of her father was a catalyst for her to connect more deeply with herself.

She says, *"the past 2-3 years since my father's passing have been transformative. I've been going to therapy and have started meditating. I quit my job, recently got married and am now thinking ahead to the next five years for my personal and professional life."*

The negative emotion Nehaarikaa most frequently feels is guilt. She also experiences anger, helplessness and sadness, especially when she witnesses human suffering. She is compassionate and has a genuine, heartfelt desire to help ease suffering.

She says, *"being helpful to others has helped me navigate the outer world. It results in better connections. I want to give hope to others with a clear action plan, especially in tough times. When there are differences in a relationship, I like to navigate a compromise. My strategy to deal with difficult situations is to not be judgmental, to go with the flow and not aim to control."*

This compassionate approach to life and others has often put Nehaarikaa in the role of a mediator and peacemaker. Although this is a gift that is much needed and appreciated, she realises that by being this type of person she is sometimes *"taking away people's agency to act on their own behalf"*.

This is a powerful insight. There is a difference between helping when someone needs and wants our help, and helping because *we think* that is what someone needs and wants. We all have a path to walk on, lessons to learn and mistakes to make. When someone steps in and points out a shortcut or offers us a lift to our destination, we are missing out on experiences that might have been crucial to our own process of becoming who we are meant to be.

If you are one of life's helpers and givers, ask yourself why you are helping. Is it really about the other person or is it to fulfil a need within yourself (that you may not be consciously aware of)? Is there a genuine need for help and, if so, are you the right person to step in? What would happen if you were not to step in?

By being habitually kind and helpful to others, deep down are you hoping someone will notice you, thank you, absolve you of some misplaced guilt, validate your efforts, be kind to you, help you and ultimately make you feel valued and loved?

It is a well-known fact that some of the kindest people project their compassion towards an external cause whilst showing utter disregard for their own wellbeing. This is an extreme kind of self-forgetting and lack of acknowledgement that they too have needs and wants.

Nehaarikaa says, *"my greatest challenge has been that I tend to judge myself. I am learning to be kinder to myself, to take a moment to reflect on my own as well as other people's points of view. I have a group of friends with whom I can really be myself and let my hair down."*

Nehaarikaa has discovered how important creating strong connections are in facilitating good communication and resolving conflict. Creating certain routines and rituals can be a really great way to ensure you don't forget what's really important. She says, *"My husband and I have certain ground rules, such as never to sleep on an argument, or walk off in anger making the other person feel abandoned. We also let go of the need to solve things right away. We will not get nasty or personal. The other ground rule is on rituals. For instance, we have a parting ritual where we see off the other person at the gate. We make time for meals together and go on dates at least once a week. We also give each other permission to vocalise how we feel. Having been friends for ten years before we got married has helped us figure out many things about each other before we got married."*

Networking

In professional settings, connecting is often described as networking. Who you know is often deemed more important than what you know. Although this sounds unfair and reeks of nepotism, you have to admit that it is often easier to work with someone you know than someone whom

PART 4

you've only just met or read/heard about. Better the devil you know, as the saying goes.

If being known matters so much, then it makes sense that we become skilled at making connections and establishing contacts. If you've avoided talking to strangers most of your life, making small talk with people you've never met may sound like your idea of hell. You might hide behind the label of being shy or being an introvert. I've heard people often use this as an excuse as to why they hate networking and view it as a necessary evil.

If you're one of life's introverts, chances are you feel drained when you go to an event with a lot of people, most of whom are strangers. The effort it takes to connect with people, engage in conversation and appear interested may be more than you can bear. You might choose to go with a colleague or a friend so you have one another for company. You might think this is a better alternative than standing in a corner by yourself wishing you'd never come. Or if you go alone, you might hide your discomfort by staring fixedly at your phone as if it were the most interesting thing in the room.

The problem with the above scenario is that you are unlikely to make any interesting or meaningful connections. Eye contact is one of the simplest and most effective ways to make a human connection. If you've come alone and decided to stand apart with your eyes on your phone, you are giving out the message "don't talk to me, I'm preoccupied". If you've come with a friend and you stick to one another, chatting away, but not looking to introduce anyone else into your conversation, you're sending the message "we're in a private conversation and you're not invited."

It will take a brave person (who is perhaps drawn to you in some way), a highly engaged host or an extrovert who loves meeting new people to come and talk to you. This means that you have ceded all control of who you connect with and might become trapped in conversation with someone who is a crashing bore or loves the sound of their own voice.

Networking for introverts

There is a common misperception that introverts are shy people and vice versa.

A shy person may not have a lot to say and might avoid situations where they are in the spotlight. Their shyness can be situational. Being around strangers and certain people might make them tongue tied, but when amongst people they know, like and trust, they may behave completely differently.

Introversion and extroversion is about give and take of emotional energy. An introvert tends to feel energy draining from them when with other people who demand their attention. Extroverts feel energised when they're with others – they exude energy but also draw energy from others. As energy is neither created nor destroyed, but rather transferred from one form to another, you can see how extroverts love being around introverts who might be good listeners. Extroverts also have the ability to raise the energy in a room so everyone feels more enlivened.

I consider myself to be an ambivert – I fall somewhere in the middle of the spectrum. I am not particularly shy, but I don't seek out the limelight. If I was in control of an event, as the host or the organiser, I have no problem being in the spotlight and ensuring my guests or audience are being taken care of. However, if I were at an event not arranged by me, where I am a participant or guest, I would show up with a very different persona: one who observes and experiences without necessarily being noticed by others. In those situations, I am drawn to one on one interactions with people who are interesting and open to meaningful conversations.

Here are my tips to networking as an introvert:

- Before you go to an event, find out what you can about it – who the organisers are, what's involved and where it is. Check in with yourself to see if what you find chimes with you.

    a. Does the event seem interesting to you?
    b. Will you learn something from it?
    c. Do you have something to offer to other attendees?
    d. Based on your own wants and needs, is it worth you investing your time and energy from start to finish (including the travel time)?

- Choose what you wear and how you look based on the impression you want to make. But whatever your choice, make sure you are comfortable with it and in it. There's nothing worse than spending the next few hours wishing your heels weren't so high, or your dress wasn't so close fitting or that you'd washed your hair. If you're a man, you might not have the same existential crises.

- Take a few deep, calming breaths, do a power pose (some people find this injects them with confidence), tell yourself you're there because you want to be and then walk in with your head held high.

- Slowly cast your eyes over the room to take in the vibe. There's no rush. Get a sense of the layout and who's there. Do you see anyone you know? If yes, they might be someone to talk to when you've caught their eye.

- Grab yourself some refreshments, if it's that sort of event. It is a good place to connect with others who are there with a similar purpose. Eye contact, a smile, a hello and let ice-breaking small talk follow. It is easier than you might think. Once you've warmed up, you can join the event knowing you've connected with at least one person.

- As an introvert, you might feel pressured to impress, know and be able to talk eloquently about all kinds of topics. This would scare most people, especially people who are not pretending they're an expert at things they know nothing about. My strategy is to get curious and take an interest in the person I've just met. Most people love to talk about themselves. They will remember you for making them feel like they are the most interesting person in the world.

We will talk more about how to communicate powerfully and with influence in our next chapter.

PART 4

Beyond human Connection

Discernment of whom to connect with, how and why is a skill that we learn through experience. Moving away from purely the logical mind and memory of past experiences, we can tap into our heart and intuition to help us decide which connections are safe and which are not. Who can be trusted, who means us harm and who might just be a lost soul craving human connection. This discernment is a muscle that gets stronger and more reliable with practice. Learning to connect in this way is a magical way to live; full of surprises and possibilities.

Over the years, I've realised that I'm one of those people who feels and reads other people's energy far better than I use my logical brain. There are empaths who feel other people's feelings and even take them on as if they were their own. I am sensitive to other people's feelings, but I am far more attuned to sensing the energy of a person, place or thing. Paying attention to how my body and mind responds to this external energy has helped me to discern if something feels right, off or just indifferent.

This sensory perception really came alive when I attended the ten-day silent meditation retreat called Vipassana that I referred to earlier in this book. The silence and non-communication allows each person to experience their meditative journey without discussion, input or interference from others who are also on that journey. Amongst other rules is one about not harming any living creatures whilst on the retreat, including the little spiders or bugs that might wander into your path. Dotted around the retreat are clear plastic cups and laminated cards. If a creepy-crawly wandered into your space uninvited, you could gently gather them up with the cup and card and release them unhurt back into the outdoors.

While on this retreat, I really noticed how different the energy of the place was. My senses were heightened by the enforced silence, the stillness and the inner peace meditation brings. Everything looked and felt more alive and vibrant. The sparse leaves on bare autumnal trees, blades of grass which seemed to implore me to tread with care, and all other forms of life seemed to connect with me. I have never experienced insects being in such a Zen state. Their energy can be described in one word: safe. It was as if they knew that in this hood no one would hurt them. At least no human would. I sensed it in how they didn't freeze or flit away in my presence, but just lazily stayed where they were. And on some core level, I connected with their feeling of safety. It moved me to tears to think how unsafe other creatures must feel in the normal outside world where these rules of non-violence towards all creatures are not followed.

Connection is about energetic awareness. Once we've learnt to connect with ourselves, connecting with the outside world becomes easier. Energy is the basis of everything, even inanimate objects. Notice how your relationship with your external environment shifts when you become aware of the energy inside and around you, and find ways to ground yourself.

PART 4

SUMMARY

As humans, we make connections with our senses and our centres of intelligence – the brain, the heart and the gut. We might use logic and prior knowledge to make sense of disparate pieces of information. We might make an emotional connection to a thing, a place, an idea or a person. And we might energetically sense if something feels right or safe or attractive for us.

In our early years, we learn how to connect with ourselves based on how others, particularly our important others, connect with us. How the people who are supposed to love us and care for us treat us becomes a template for how we treat ourselves in later life.

Knowing yourself, why you are the way you are and how certain events make you feel is such an important step towards freedom. What you do with that knowledge and how you interact with the outside world is equally important. How we connect with others without losing ourselves in the process is key to living an abundant life.

As young children, unfiltered connections came naturally to us. Social conditioning and life experiences make us wary and selective in our interactions. A stranger is simply a person you don't yet know. One of them could one day become a best friend, a life partner, a mentor or teacher or a guardian angel in your time of need.

Of course, not every relationship will be right for you. You can learn to read the signs and discern a "good" connection from a "bad" one, a healthy relationship from a damaging one. This kind of discernment is easier when you really know yourself, what you need and want, and what your core values are.

In professional settings, connecting is often described as networking. If you're an introvert, chances are you feel drained when you go to an event with a lot of people, most of whom are strangers. You can try my simple tips for a great networking experience even if you are an introvert. These include being intentional about the kinds of events you choose to attend, sensing and reading the room, and following your curiosity.

When we understand that connection is an energetic awareness, it is easy to see that it extends well beyond humans. Once we've learnt to connect with ourselves, connecting with the outside world becomes easier. Energy is the basis of everything, even inanimate objects. Notice how your relationship with your external environment shifts when you become aware of the energy inside and around you, and find ways to ground yourself.

EXERCISES

Here's a simple and powerful way to connect with yourself. Find a place where you can sit comfortably and undisturbed. Close your eyes and take a few calming rhythmic breaths. Imagine there is beautiful golden light hovering just in front of your closed eyes. Feel this light enter your body along with your next in-breath. Now imagine the light takes your attention by the hand and they both get on to the carriage of your breath. With the help of this guiding light, your attention travels to different parts of your body and becomes a compassionate observer. Notice what you find and pay attention to what your body is trying to convey to you.

Try one or more of these exercises to help you connect more deeply with your inner and outer world:

1. Pick a positive emotion and do a body scan to discover where in your body you most feel this emotion. For instance, if the emotion is peace, find out how peace somatically manifests for you.

2. Pick a negative emotion, perhaps one you are familiar with, and do a body scan. Where in your body does this emotion show itself? Does it have any less obvious hiding places?

3. Connect with your inner child. Find a photo of your younger self – one in which you were still

innocent to the ways of the world. Imprint that image in your mind and then close your eyes and emotionally connect with the younger you. At first, you don't have to say anything – simply be there for your younger self and see what emerges.

4. Connect with someone you love or know well. It could be your significant other, parent, sibling or child. Do this entirely through your thoughts and feelings. Hold an image of the person in your mind and send loving thoughts their way. Such as, I love you, I appreciate you, I am grateful for all you do, I am sorry I upset you, etc.

5. Connect with an animal – it could be one that is part of your family, or an animal you see on TV, or even a dog you walk past on the street. Hold the image of the animal and send positive thoughts their way. Such as, you are loved, your presence matters, you are beautiful, etc.

6. Connect with the inanimate objects in your life. Whether it is your car, your home, your sofa, your bed or even your phone. Look at it and express your gratitude for how they make your life better via your thoughts.

7. Connect with your imagination and the vision you see of the kind of life you want to live. Tune into the frequency of this world you see in your mind's eye until it feels real and happening in the present moment.

5.

Communication

 YAY!

 GRRR...

 SAD!

 *GULP*

 *SNORES*

ANXIETY
BOREDOM
COPING

Body Language

DEPRESSION
EMBARRASMENT
FIGHT-or-FLIGHT

> *"The most important thing in communication is hearing what isn't said."*
>
> **PETER DRUCKER**

We communicate in many different ways. We consciously use language to convey our thoughts and feelings both verbally and in writing. Studies conducted by Dr Mehrabian suggested that only 7% of all communication is verbal (language and the words we use), 55% is visual (body language and facial expressions), and 38% is vocal (pitch, tone, cadence and modulation of the voice). Whether you agree with those precise percentages or not, most of our communication is non-verbal and occurs in ways that we might not be conscious of.

In his book, *The Man Who Mistook His Wife for a Hat,* the renowned neurologist and author Oliver Sacks tells a story that illustrates how cognitive dissonance occurs when the words don't match the body language. In his chapter "The President's Speech" he describes a hospital ward for patients with Aphasia, a neurological disorder that leaves the sufferer devoid of language, and unable to speak or understand words. Aphasiacs rely almost completely on non-verbal cues that occur naturally, often without conscious intent. President Ronald Reagan's much awaited speech was on TV, full of rhetoric and theatrics, as was his oratory style. To the Aphasiacs the President could just as well have been doing a stand-up comedy routine, for most of them roared with laughter. There was nothing amusing in his speech, and yet something about his body language had sent them a very different message. The same is true of babies and animals who don't understand verbal language but can accurately interpret visual, vocal and emotional cues.

The science of communication

All communication is an energetic flow once a connection has been made. Positive emotions such as peace, love, joy and gratitude have a higher vibration, whilst negative emotions such as anger, fear, hatred and shame have a lower vibration. Our bodies react differently in the presence of a joyful or calm person than when interacting with someone who is angry, agitated or very sad.

Have you ever considered how your body is impacted by your own thoughts and feelings? You communicate with yourself in the same way you might with the outside world, except that others can't hear your thoughts like your body can. When you're being particularly harsh, self-critical and even downright cruel in ways you are thinking or judging yourself, your body has no way of getting away from the onslaught.

There is a constant communication happening between our body, our senses and our centres of intelligence. Only the body is truly listening and taking on board every little nuance of what is being communicated. Our bodies are taking in and storing our every word, thought and feeling, and every sensory stimulus and experience.

Social conditioning and over-reliance on verbal language makes us forget, or override, what we've always known. If we are to become better communicators, we must learn to pay attention to what is being said when there are no words. I had an unforgettable experience in 2020 that powerfully demonstrated to me how we can communicate with parts of the body, exactly as if it were a sentient being (which of course it is).

It was during one of the Covid lockdowns in 2020. My then husband was in hospital with a serious illness and, as his next of kin, I was the only person allowed to visit. The doctors and nurses were taking almost daily blood samples to assess his progress. His arms were covered in bruises from all the poking and jabbing with needles.

On one of my daily visits, I was told that they'd been unsuccessful at drawing a blood sample that day. The nurses had unsuccessfully tried different veins and used various tactics to get them to open up. While I was there, a doctor arrived to check on him. He, too, tried to draw a sample of blood but to no avail. I asked him why it was proving a problem today. He said, *"because we've been drawing small amounts each day, the veins are closing up for fear of too much blood being taken. They are doing this to protect the body. Of course, your husband is in no danger as we're only taking small amounts each time, which poses no threat."*

As I took in this information, I stood on the other side of the bed and held my husband's hand as the doctor tried again. I closed my eyes and visualised my husband's veins. I felt their fear. I saw their fierce courage in closing the door to any more blood being taken. I was moved. Through my thoughts I connected with them with compassion. I assured them that there was no danger. I explained that these blood samples were there to check how his healing was progressing. I thanked them for the work they did and for protecting him. I requested for them to open up so that the sample could be taken and no further poking and prodding would be necessary, at least not today. To my amazement, seconds later the doctor exclaimed that the vein had opened up and the blood was flowing freely into his vial.

Of course, I have no scientific evidence to prove that this is what really happened. It is possible the veins just got a bit fed up with being repeatedly prodded, the medical personnel not accepting no for an answer, and decided to open up in tired resignation.

Whatever your viewpoint, I was stunned at the possibility that I had just communicated with the veins in my husband's body! I was aware of healing through visualisation and used it on myself all the time. But I had never experienced such instantaneous communication and response with another person's body before. And if that is possible, then it confirms we communicate with other living things through our thoughts and intentions.

Interspecies Communication

We are also constantly communicating with other species of living beings, including plants and animals. We may not be aware of what they're saying to us or how they're feeling, but they can see right through us. They may not understand the words we use, but they are fluent in the language of the energy behind our words, our thoughts and intentions.

In 2018, the Swedish retailer IKEA conducted an experiment on plants at a school as part of their anti-bullying campaign. They placed two identical plants in a communal area of the school. Over a period of 30 days, the students were invited to say complimentary things to one plant, and mean things to the other. In every other way – light, water and nutrition – both plants were treated the same. After 30 days, the plant that received compliments was healthy and thriving, whilst the other one looked sad and droopy. The plants are unlikely to have understood the words, but they seemingly responded to the feelings behind the words.

I watched a fascinating documentary in which South African interspecies communicator Anna Breytenbach communicates with animals in the wild. In it the presenter follows Anna as she fearlessly joins a troop of baboons who'd had a difficult relationship with humans and were known to be aggressive. Within minutes she gained their trust and it seemed as if they unburdened their weary hearts to her with stories of tragic consequences of their interactions with humans. Most memorably, at a wild cat sanctuary, she connected and communicated with a beautiful but very dangerous black leopard named Diablo who was having a hard time trusting humans. You have to watch it to believe the transformation from an angry and mistrustful beast into a majestic and gentle one. All because he felt understood and was able to communicate what he wanted.

Anna communicates, not just with animals, but also plants. Those of you who are vegetarian or vegan might be dismayed to learn that plants, too, experience joy and pain, don't enjoy being factory farmed and have heartbreaking stories to tell. Her approach is calm and respectful. She becomes very still and totally present to receiving communication from the animals and plants in whatever way they choose to send it. She believes that every one of us has the ability to do what she does. All we need is a bit of guidance and practice.

What hinders most of us from communicating at this pure spiritual level is the deafening noise of our thoughts, our prejudices and the sounds of a busy world. Listen and silent have the same letters. True listening happens from a place of stillness and silence. Not just auditory silence, but the quieting of the endless mental chatter. We really hear when we open our senses and let the messages reach us unfiltered.

Rose

Rose has kept a journal since she was in the sixth grade. She was inspired by her mother who used to keep a diary as a chronicle of the day's events. Journaling was how Rose connected with what was going on inside her. She says, *"it gives me a lot of comfort. As I write, I am able to process my thoughts and feelings. Journaling has been a constant in my life. I feel uncomfortable if I don't journal."*

Rose grew up in a Catholic family that went to church every Sunday. She says, *"I've always been an optimist. I believe that if you really want something, the universe will conspire to help you. If life is throwing a challenge at you, it is because it has equipped you with the wherewithal to deal with it. This way of thinking gave me hope, optimism and confidence all through my childhood and adolescence."*

Journaling has helped Rose become more aware of her physical and mental health. She says, *"I started tracking my menstrual cycle and my energy levels at different points in the cycle. It has helped me be more proactive in how I choose to expend energy. When my energy levels are low, I give myself permission to curl up in bed and rest."*

The negative emotions Rose most frequently experiences are disappointment and irritation. She adds, *these are directed mostly at myself for not doing enough,* "and at my husband when he doesn't do what I've asked him to do. The greatest disappointment for me is the realisation *that I do a lot of things that are not meaningful. Having my personal values aligned with the organisation I work for is really important to me. Intellectual stimulation alone is not enough."* Journaling helps, but she admits that she finds it easier to let go of disappointments others have caused her than the self-inflicted ones.

Her deep connection with herself and the regular communication through journaling has helped her get very clear on what truly matters to her. *"One of my core values is that time is the most precious of gifts. The time you give to people is more important than the things you give them. I value experiences over things. I want to be light on the planet and buy things that are good for you, such as organic food."*

Rose says she doesn't compare herself to others anymore, but she does wistfully look back at who she once was. She is aware of the impact she has on others and knows she has the potential to be so much more.

She says, *"when I was growing up I was an optimistic and courageous person. Over the years I've got bogged down by constraints and become a meeker version of myself. I wish I could believe I have more power to control what happens in my life. At times I behave as if I have no agency and put constraints in my life. I should test the constraints and give myself permission to stretch a bit more. I don't want to upset the status quo, especially with my children. Am I being lazy? Am I using my children as an excuse?"*

People who listen to their own thoughts and feelings with equanimity and compassion have generally learnt to be truly present. This can make them good listeners who can make others feel heard.

PART 4

Rose says, *"when it comes to the outer world, I am a good listener; I am interested in people and their stories. I am not conscious of who I become when I am with others, but I sense it later. I sense that I am different with different people."* But she admits that she doesn't always get it right in a conflict situation. She says, *"I find it is easier to communicate with strangers, but it can be harder to communicate with the people who are close to you. I struggle to communicate with my husband and my eleven-year-old son. A lack of coherent communication can prevent me from resolving conflict. I can be blunt, which doesn't often go down well. I have to find better ways of disagreeing. Saying 'no' or pushing back in a nicer way is a work-in-progress for me."*

Finding the right tone and words can be difficult when you are going from one situation into another completely different one. Let's say you've had a stressful conversation with your boss and now you're having to meet your friends for a drink, it might take a while for you to switch mental and emotional gears. These are called transitions, and we can learn how to navigate them. We can do this by acknowledging that one event has ended. To take stock of it, accept and process it if possible, calm the mind before moving on to the next event. The aim is to avoid hangovers from previous experiences, to be completely present and take stock of each situation and respond accordingly.

Rose offers an example that most parents might resonate with. *"It was a Monday morning when my children were both dragging their heels and complaining about going to school. Normally, I might have lost my temper and got stressed about them being late for their school bus. But on that occasion, I was feeling calmer and took the time to ask my son why he didn't want to go to school. Listen-*

ing to him and acknowledging his feelings made him feel seen and understood. He left for school and I felt proud at how I had handled the situation, how I stepped back before things escalated. I saw at that moment that the distress of my child was more important than my need to get him out of the house."

How to communicate more effectively

People who want to communicate better often enrol themselves into elocution lessons or public speaking classes. Not many people are taking courses on how to listen better or how to read body language. Listening and noticing visual cues is such an important part of communication. So many misunderstandings and conflicts might be averted if we paid more attention to all aspects of communication and checked we have correctly understood what is being conveyed.

Here are a few simple rules to better communication:

1. **Be clear about your purpose**
   Maybe you're at a networking event and you're there to meet potential clients or suppliers. Be clear about your reasons for being there and what you hope to achieve through your interactions. Or you might be the host at a meeting, in which case the same applies.

2. **Be interested and open minded**
   Take a genuine interest in the person you are speaking to. Ask mostly open-ended questions that invite them to talk about things that are relevant to your purpose and the reason they are there. However much you think you know, go in with a beginner's mindset and stay open to learning something new.

3. **Be fully present**
   Engage your full attention. Listen. Look and be interested. Reflect back to make sure you understand. Ask follow-up questions. People are more likely to remember you if you made them feel seen, heard and understood. Don't let your mind or your eyes wander. They will sense they've lost you.

4. **Be non-judgmental**
   If you've ever watched professionals in an improv performance, you will notice how effortlessly they keep the flow going even when the most ludicrous, even disagreeable, things are said. Phrases such as "I can see why you might think that" or "I see it differently" or "You might be right" are better than making definitive statements, such as "I disagree" or "You are wrong". Use of "Yes, and" is also preferred to words such as "No, but." Negative words act like roadblocks and put the other person on the defensive.

5. **Be interesting and congruent**
   When it's your turn to speak, whether it is to ask a question or to share an opinion, be clear and concise. Convey your message in a way that would make sense to your audience. Use humour if appropriate. Be aware of the pitch, tone and pace of your voice, as well as your body language. Ensure congruence with your words, i.e. if you are saying something serious, saying it with a big smile on your face and too much hand movement may create cognitive dissonance. Pay attention to the non-verbal cues of your audience. Give them space to ask questions and also change tack if you sense your message is not landing with them.

SUMMARY

We communicate in many different ways. We consciously use language to convey our thoughts and feelings both verbally and in writing. Studies conducted by Dr Mehrabian suggested that only 7% of all communication is verbal (language and the words we use), 55% is visual (body language and facial expressions), and 38% is vocal (pitch, tone, cadence and modulation of the voice).

All communication is the flow of energy once a connection has been made. Positive emotions such as peace, love, joy and gratitude have a higher vibration, whilst negative emotions such as anger, fear, hatred and shame have a lower vibration. Our bodies react differently in the presence of a joyful or calm person than when interacting with someone who is angry, agitated or very sad.

There is a constant communication happening between our body, our senses and our centres of intelligence. Our bodies are taking in and storing our every word, thought and feeling, and every sensory stimulus and experience. If we are to become better communicators, we must learn to pay attention to what is being said when there are no words.

Have you ever considered how your body is impacted by your own thoughts and feelings? You communicate with yourself in the same way you might with the outside world, except that others can't hear your thoughts like your body can. When you're being particularly harsh, self-critical and even downright cruel in ways you are thinking or judging yourself, your body has no way of getting away from the onslaught.

PART 4

We also communicate with other species of living beings, including plants and animals. We may not be aware of what they're saying to us or what they're feeling, but they can see right through us. They may not understand the words we use, but they are fluent in the language of the energy behind our words, our thoughts and intentions.

People who want to communicate better often enrol themselves into elocution lessons or public speaking classes. Not many people are taking courses on how to listen better, to become really present or how to read body language. Listening and noticing visual cues is such an important part of communication. So many misunderstandings and conflicts might be averted if we paid more attention to all aspects of communication and checked we have correctly understood what is being conveyed.

EXERCISES

Remember, we are communicating all the time. Even if we are standing still and not saying a word. Our very being is energetically sending messages, and our body is speaking a language that is far more powerful than the words we are choosing to speak or withhold.

Try one of these each day of the week, in different situations and in varying emotional states. The purpose is to become aware of your own natural style of communication and make changes that are right for you and feel authentically yours.

1. Notice the language of your thoughts. On average, what is the ratio of compliments and kind words vs. judgement and criticism?

2. Pay attention to your own body language and facial gestures. Do you notice any correlation between how you are feeling and the messages your body is sending you and the outside world? For instance, do you tense up or cross your arms when you are feeling stressed?

3. Observe the tone, volume and cadence of your voice in different situations. How do you sound when you are relaxed and happy? What about when you are feeling annoyed or anxious? Remember, if you are on the phone, your voice is all the person at the other end has to go by in terms of your non-verbal communication.

4. Become mindful of the words you use to talk to and about yourself. Words matter, even if only a small portion of our overall communication. Imagine that when you are talking to yourself, you are communicating with the child you once were. If you are in the habit of saying things like, "I'm such an idiot! I never do anything right. I don't know why I bother", consider how your inner child feels upon hearing these words. How would this new awareness change how you talk to yourself?

5. Practise active listening and being fully present (even when communicating with yourself) without feeling the need to judge or jump in with comments or advice. Listening to the silent language of your body is one of the greatest gifts you will give yourself.

6. Notice how you react to different styles of communication from others. Your body and your subconscious mind is very good at discerning who and what is right for you, even if you are not consciously aware. Aligning your awareness with this inner knowing will help you make better choices and interact with the outer world more effectively.

7. Notice how others react to your different styles of communication. A similar awareness of the effect you have on others will help you make a choice on whether you are with the right people, or if you need to change the way you are around them.

6.

PART 4

When you live in a world where there is freedom and choice, there will inevitably be differences. People can't be expected to think or feel the same way, to want the same things or behave in an identical manner, especially not in a democratic society that prizes individuality. In fact, the whole concept of diversity and inclusion relies on a willingness to embrace differences. When done well, these differences make the value of the whole greater than the sum of the parts.

Conflict arises when there is a misalignment of opinions, expectations, goals or actions that can then lead to disagreements or clashes. For some people, creating conflict is the only way they can draw attention to themselves or the cause they represent. They'll do anything to be noticed, to be taken seriously, to be understood.

It is natural to become attached to our own point of view. Anyone who questions or presents an alternative viewpoint can make us feel uncomfortable. They are disruptors who shake us out of the status quo and force us to consider a different way of doing things. There can be no transformation without disruption.

In the face of conflict, there are a few different responses: fight, flight, freeze or flow. There is no right or wrong; it depends on the nature of the threat or disruption. However, it is important to be aware of what is your default response to adversity.

Is your default response to fight back and bludgeon the dissenter into submission or scare them away? This may give you the satisfaction of winning but consider the wider implication of this. You may be viewed as a bully. People might be too afraid to give you bad news or disagree with you. You might be surrounded by yes-people over whom you have forceful control.

If your default response is to flee, i.e. you avoid conflict by either physically removing yourself from unpleasant situations or by mentally dissociating from them, you are foregoing opportunities to express your point of view, which might be a valuable one. In effect, you are letting the other side get their own way unchallenged. There may come a time when you realise you no longer have a seat at the table where big decisions are made because you are viewed as passive or indifferent.

If your default option is to freeze, then consider a secondary question. Is freezing giving you time to really consider what's going on before you make your next move? Or does it send you into a state of paralysing indecisiveness? Unless you're in an emergency situation where freezing could mean life or death, I would advocate that more of us "freeze" a little during situations that have the potential to escalate into full blown conflict. The pause might cool things down, create space and time for everyone to consider what really matters and proceed in a more constructive way.

If your default option is to flow then ask yourself how often you go with someone else's flow because you don't know what you want, or are afraid of creating conflict. There are many advantages of being a flowy person: you see other people's perspective, you don't take sides and can be a very useful mediator. But you need to know when to step aside when your work is done. And it can be really powerful when you can influence the direction of the flow to create a better outcome for everyone.

The internal conflict

What happens when your head, heart and gut want very different things? Which of the three centres of intelligence dominates your decision making? And how does your body handle the conflict this creates in your life? How often do you take the time and space to check in with the less dominant ones?

Every day you are having to make choices based on imprecise information and situations that are far from perfect. Your head might struggle to offer clear direction, the heart will view it through an emotional lens, and the gut might be sending signals in a language you don't understand. This kind of internal conflict is every bit as uncomfortable as the conflict we face with others. The only difference is, it might be easier to numb ourselves to what's going on inside us.

We experience internal conflict every time we are not completely present to life. We may be physically present, going through the motions, but our mind is elsewhere, our heart longs for something else and our gut is telling us that we are wasting our time.

Dhanashree

Dhanashree greatly values her time and has learnt not to invest time on people who don't care for her or her time. One of the ways Dhanashree manages her time is by assessing how urgent and/or important something is. And when she deems it not worthy of her time or effort, she has learned to delegate. She adds, *"the formula that works for me is this: when you delegate and the standard of the work is acceptable (even if not exceptional), don't criticise it. Make peace with it."*

Dhanashree admits that she's not great at gauging if someone is trustworthy or not, so she plays cautious until she is sure. She says, *"When I'm with people I don't trust, I use the minimum number of words. I use the technique you'd use with a lawyer in a courtroom! I don't argue. I don't try to prove I'm right. I end the conversation with the words 'maybe you're right'."*

Dhanashree believes that *"conflicts happen because two parties don't agree, either due to ego issues, a difference of opinion, a lack of awareness or because there's been a misunderstanding. If both parties have the same intent and desire the same outcome, conflict can be resolved."* Disagreeing with someone without being disagreeable is an important way to have honest and open conversations without them turning into a conflict or confrontation.

She says, *"there are two kinds of conflict – one of which you are a part of and the other where you are mediating conflict between others. I used to run away from conflict, but now I have learnt to deal with it better. In professional settings, I assess if it is worth my time. If the answer is yes, I take it to the next level. If the conflict is with someone higher up, I assess the cost vs. benefit of escalating it. I will ask for a 1-1 meeting with that person to understand what they want and how we can work together. In personal situations, I first establish my own boundaries and assess where the other person's boundaries lie. Knowing where the boundaries lie can be hard."*

Getting clear on our own boundaries, and learning to respect other people's boundaries, is one of the best ways to resolve conflicts.

Why we avoid conflict

Most people dislike conflict. It feels unpleasant. It can escalate and get blown out of proportion. It brings out uncomfortable emotions like anger, resentment, blame and hatred. It disrupts the status quo. It shatters the peace and creates ill will.

Four years ago, a client of mine introduced me to the Enneagram – an ancient study of personality types. She sent me a video of Richard Rohr painting a picture of each type at an Enneagram Conference. I was transfixed. Here, at last, was an explanation for why I was the way I was.

Unlike other personality typing systems that label you based on your behavioural patterns, the Enneagram goes deeper. It helps you see why you are the way you are. It introduces you to your gifts as well as your limitations. It shows you how, if you're not careful, your gifts become your limitations. More importantly, it connects you with the child you once were and what made you the adult you now are. Far from putting you in your personality type box, it offers tools to get out of the box and learn from the other types who are not like you.

As I burrowed down the Enneagram rabbit hole, for the first time I really understood why certain patterns recurred in my life. I discovered that peace and harmony have always been more important to me than almost anything else. This has been a gift in many ways. I am a live-and-let-live kind of person. I go with the flow and have a gift of putting people at ease. The flipside of this is that in order to keep the peace I go to great lengths to deflect and avoid conflict.

Compromise has played a big role, especially in my personal life where the stakes are always the highest and I long for a harmonious life. Compromise is generally a good thing. It is the basis of peaceful societies, and we could do with more of it in our current social-media fuelled fractious world. The true meaning of compromise is an agreement that is reached when *both sides* make concessions. In mathematical terms, a perfect compromise might be when you meet each other halfway. Reality is never this exact, but over time the give and take should feel equitable.

Keeping the peace by constantly giving in to the demands of another is not a true compromise. It is a subjugation of one's own needs and desires in order to not rock the boat. You might give in to every unreasonable demand because there is a mismatched power dynamic. Or you fear that if you don't the other person might deprive you of something only they can give you. There might be a fear of abandonment, of not being loved, of being harassed, of them hurting someone you care about very much. You will do anything to not let your fears come to pass.

When you do this all the time it takes a toll on your body and spirit. Every such caving in adds a layer of anger and helplessness at the unfairness of it all. Every such disproportionate concession adds to the feeling that you are not important, what you think, feel and want matters less than someone else's will.

In my case, it was more subtle. It wasn't about a massive power mismatch either, and I did not tick most of the boxes of someone who might bend to someone else's unjust will, but I had learnt early on that I needed to pick my battles and conserve my energy for things worth fighting for. So, I'd make a quick mental calculation about whether a potential conflict or confrontation was worth the disruption to my inner equanimity and status quo. This was generally a good strategy. I didn't sweat the small stuff. It made for a more peaceful life.

I only realised much later, when the dysfunctionality within my family came to the fore, what I considered "small stuff" was the steady erosion of the little things that mattered to my family, but I could not see. Perhaps I chose not to see because not seeing was less disruptive to my inner peace. Over time, this benign neglect affected me and my family deeply. The effect on me went unnoticed at first until the strands of resentment, loneliness and disappointment manifested in the form of a frozen shoulder and other health issues. I know now that peace at any cost is not worth it. It is an uneasy truce that stores up bigger problems further down the line.

Making peace with conflict

Such well-intentioned peacekeeping is also detrimental to the person who is optically "winning". By offering no resistance to their irrational behaviour and actions, we've inadvertently sent them the message that we agree with them, or that we haven't got it in us to stand up to them, or that we are indifferent to them and their behaviour.

Letting someone repeatedly get their own way crowds out other potential approaches and ideas that might have been really good for everyone. It creates the bystander effect where you've turned a blind eye to events that in your heart you know should not be happening.

This sort of mutely standing by happens in professional settings when you're faced with someone who is very opinionated and forceful. There may be a power dynamic that makes it hard for you to speak up, even if you profoundly disagree. The cost of dissent may be higher than you are willing to bear. You might regret the last time you spoke up only to be ignored or belittled, especially in front of their peers. The bully gets away with it again and your self-esteem takes a beating.

With every such diminishment of self-worth, you are storing up greater levels of stress and dissatisfaction. Life can be hellish when you believe that avoiding conflict is the only way to keep your job or to keep your family together.

Whether it's in your personal life or in professional settings, you will come across people who like to forcefully assert their will in order to be in control. We can't change how others behave, but we can evaluate what makes us tick and how we can respond better. The aim should be to make constructive peace, not to keep an illusion of peace at any cost.

Darshana

We met Darshana earlier in Part 2 of this book. Her curious and open nature means she is very good at making connections and interacting with a range of people. She says, "*I am myself in all interactions, but there are different sides to me that people I've connected with at different stages in my life have seen and experienced. I don't try to impress people.*"

Connecting with people in an authentic and mindful way makes it easier when it comes to communication. Darshana was in a marriage that didn't last long. Looking back on it she can see she learnt a great many lessons. She gained a better understanding of her own non-negotiable values, what her triggers are and what she is looking for in a life partner. And she got really good at managing conflict.

PART 4

This is her philosophy around managing conflict. *"If we don't agree with a certain point, we agree to disagree and not let it escalate. If someone is upset with me, I apologise for the way I made them feel even if I still disagree with them. Discussing over a call is so much better. In person is best, then on call, and the last choice is texting."*

If you've ever endured a lengthy text battle, you will agree that it is a fruitless and sometimes aggravating way to communicate when there's a disagreement. It relies purely on the words on the screen – words that are so often autocorrected and not at all what you intended. Words that might be devoid of emotion (unless you're an accomplished writer). This mode of communication relies on the texter being able to articulate in words what they are trying to convey as quickly as your fingers have learnt to type. Instant communication has created an expectation of immediacy. Where time and space might have allowed tempers to cool, the instant back and forth can instead fuel the fire.

What is even worse than a heated text battle is when the aggrieved person's texts are met with stony silence. They have no way of knowing what the recipient is thinking or why they're staying silent. It is a hurtful way to treat someone you care about. It creates all kinds of demons and scenarios in the other person's mind, which only aggravates their sense of distress. It can be reminiscent of childhood experiences of parental emotional unavailability that felt like abandonment.

Darshana has a place on her phone where she keeps lists, reminders and notes about people she's met. That last bit is so helpful if, like me, you have a memory like a sieve and struggle with names and other identifying details. She also has a separate section with notes about things she wants to discuss with her partner. She says, *"when I have something important I want to discuss with him, I wait until it is the right time even if it eats me up from within. By not immediately engaging and showing him my irritation, it allows space and time before we have the conversation. It removes the emotion and gives me clarity. The conversation becomes more rational and cool headed. The insecurity, the anger etc are parked somewhere else. Usually we want an immediate resolution. By being patient and finding the right time you get a better result."*

This is great relationship advice. It is a highly effective way of bringing a grievance or disagreement to the table in a measured and conversational way, rather than it turning into an emotionally charged blame game.

Constructive ways of dealing with conflict

Here are a few things I've learnt about dealing with conflict in a more purposeful and constructive way.

1. Begin with a conversation, not confrontation

Much of a potential conflict begins in our minds and is based on what our body has come to expect. Perhaps in the past you've faced resistance or a flat refusal when you've asked for something. Now, when you really want something, your body is remembering how asking for it usually led to feelings of disappointment and resentment. Now, even though you are older and the power dynamic is different, you go into the situation expecting resistance, and therefore tactically take a slightly more assertive stance from the outset. It might give off the message that I want this and I'm not taking no for an answer, and if your answer is no, I intend to go ahead and do it anyway. The person might have had no objections to your request, but your prematurely confrontational manner might put them on edge.

When I was growing up, life was good even if we didn't own a lot of stuff. My father was in the Indian Navy and my stay-at-home mother was very skilled at making my father's modest earnings last from month to month. My brother and I never lacked the important things in life, but toys and treats were a rarity. I got so used to my mum saying, "No, you can't have that because it is too expensive" that after a while I just stopped asking. In this way I entirely avoided any conflict and disappointment.

However controversial the request, it is a good idea to always begin with a simple conversation, preferably without preconceptions around how someone might respond. Go into the conversation with an open mind and you may be surprised to find you are more aligned with the other person than you think.

2. Invite multiple perspectives

In every situation there are at least as many perspectives as there are people who are party to it. When we really want something, or don't want something, our point of view might feel like the most important one. Our attention might become focused on making others see why our idea, our need, our direction is the one they should accept. We might be in a hurry to get things over the line. Any dithering or resistance feels like delaying tactics put there only to thwart us. We might assert our will and use our power to get our own way. But chances are the support will be half-hearted or conditional. This is the push approach to leading, not the pull approach that is ultimately more powerful.

It's like the story of blindfolded individuals who were led to an elephant and then asked to identify what it was based on the part of the elephant's body they were allowed to touch. We all have blind spots and limitations that prevent us from seeing the full picture, and from seeing things the way others see them. This includes how we view ourselves. We don't always see ourselves the way others see us. If we did, we might behave differently.

Create space and time for people to verbally ventilate and express how they think and feel about the matter in question. Make them feel seen and heard. Look at things from different angles and perspectives. This approach not only allows for a more thorough exploration of the problem and its consequences, but it is also more likely to result in a solution that is superior to the original one.

3. Get clear on intentions and desired outcomes

Many conflicts are utterly unnecessary, especially when it becomes clear that both parties want the same things but have different ideas of how to get there. Some conflicts go on for so long that no one remembers why they began in the first place.

Before engaging in any actual or potential conflict, it is very important to get clear on what you really want – both as a final outcome and now as a consequence of your engagement. Without clarity on this, how can you know what you are fighting for? How will you know you've been successful, or indeed how much longer you need to keep going? How can you judge whether you've allocated sufficient attention and resources to the task?

Things can spiral out of control when people react rather than respond. Reactions typically come from a place of unconscious habits and old memories. A cocked eyebrow combined with a faint smile might trigger memories of being mocked. It might trigger you to react defensively or even with anger. A certain tone of voice might take you back to past events when you were made to feel small and powerless. This might cause you to react in a way that is not congruent with what's really going on. Reactions happen before we've had a chance to assess the situation consciously and calmly.

On the other hand, responses are considered and can be commensurate with the stimulus presented to us. In his bestselling memoir *Man's Search for Meaning* Viktor Frankl says, *"Between stimulus and response there is a space. In that space is our power to choose our response. In our response lies our growth and our freedom."* Freedom from the shackles of our past and the emotional baggage we carry.

When you feel triggered, it is helpful to pause and to consciously take in the current reality. It can help to put some distance between you and the stimulus before taking a calming few breaths and reminding yourself why you are there, what you want to achieve and what response will maximise your chances of getting there. Get clear on your intentions and desired outcomes.

4. Get clear on boundaries and non-negotiables

Internal and external conflict often arises when we are not getting the things we want. It could be a better job, a more loving relationship, external validation or more financial security. Not receiving this creates inner turmoil and, as we take action to achieve the things we want, we may encounter resistance or even hostility.

People with porous or non-existent boundaries get pushed around in the name of peace. Even if you are not sure of what you really want, you will have a pretty good idea of what you don't want. Resolving conflicts requires give and take. Will you know how much is too much? What values and core beliefs will you need to be aware of when you accept a deal?

Let's take the example of someone who really wants to be considered for promotion. She's tried asking for it but had been batted away and told she wasn't ready. No further reasons are given. Meanwhile, several newer colleagues who are less experienced than her are making steady progress. On paper there is every reason for her to have got the promotion. She is bringing in the business and clients trust her. During one candid conversation with a senior member of the management team she expresses her disappointment at not having made more progress. In an unguarded moment, he tells her that the role she is going after requires a lot of after-hours schmoozing and socialising with clients, spending time entertaining them and hand-holding them through difficult times. The management doesn't think she would be ready, willing or able to put in the extra hours. On reflection, she agrees. To her, quality time with her family is more important than babysitting her clients day and night.

Now that she has clarity of what's really required of the role and where her boundaries lie, she decides to apply for a job elsewhere.

In the above example, there was internal conflict, but external conflict was avoided by gaining clarity on what she'd have to give up in order to receive the prize that was the promotion.

5. Negotiate with the big picture in mind

I'm not a fan of hard-nosed negotiation, the kind you see in the movies or on Wall Street. I much prefer the kind where both sides have a chance to explore what they really want, what they're prepared to let go and where their boundaries lie. Often having a third party who acts as a mediator or objective observer can help create a more level playing field.

A good friend of mine who runs negotiation workshops told me about a time when he was asked to help a client whose team members were in a state of internal conflict. The original UK version of *The Office*, with Ricky Gervais playing the character of the boss, is a great parody on the bitchiness that pervades office politics. The them and us. The casual put downs and belittling of the work done by people in a different department. The mistaken belief that only what you do is important and everyone else is an overpaid idiot. A similar dynamic was at play here, and there was a palpable lack of mutual respect based largely on ignorance and self-aggrandisement.

My friend's approach was simple. He got the people concerned to go and shadow one another for a week. Each team member got a much better sense of what their colleague did over their working day, the challenges they faced, the limitations they contended with and, most of all, how it felt to be doing that job. When they returned to the negotiating table, he asked each team member to put himself or herself in the shoes of the other and outline what they would do to resolve the impasse.

The results were astounding. By looking at things from the perspective of others in the business, they could see the big picture and the challenges they each faced. When each person felt more seen and understood by their colleagues, they themselves became more willing to do the same for others. Where before they only cared about their little unit and how it performed, they now saw themselves as part of a bigger entity with a shared purpose and goal. It's the difference between being part of an orchestra vs. being a solo performer. You don't have to be perfect, but you do need to be in sync and harmony with the other players in order to create beautiful music.

6. Make clear agreements

The absence of ambiguity is key when it comes to making solid, watertight agreements. The five steps we've already talked about will help to create a sound foundation. We've approached things with an open mind, laid bare the issue that is causing contention, looked at it from multiple perspectives, clearly signposted our own and others' intentions and goals, understood the limitations and boundaries and talked about possible solutions.

Now it's time to put it all down in clear and concise terms; what it means for the way forward and what the goals are, what each person is required to do, what they can expect from you and one another, and what the consequences are of non-compliance with the terms of the agreement.

In everyday life we often think we've made an agreement with someone, but really what we've done is that we've unilaterally decided what needs to happen. We might expect them to behave in certain ways or achieve certain outcomes, but they are blissfully unaware. Most people are not good at mind reading. By not clearly communicating our expectations we are inviting disappointment. This in itself becomes a source of future conflict.

SUMMARY

When you live in a world where there is freedom and choice, there will inevitably be differences. People can't be expected to think or feel the same way, to want the same things or behave in an identical manner, especially not in a democratic society that prizes individuality. In fact, the whole concept of diversity and inclusion relies on a willingness to embrace differences. When done well, these differences make the value of the whole greater than the sum of the parts.

Conflict arises when there is a misalignment of opinions, expectations, goals or actions that can then lead to disagreements or clashes. In the face of conflict, there are a few different responses: fight, flight, freeze or flow. There is no right or wrong; it depends on the nature of the threat or disruption. However, it is important to be aware of what is your default response to adversity.

What happens when your head, heart and gut want very different things? Which of the three centres of intelligence dominates your decision making? And how does your body handle the conflict this creates in your life? How often do you take the time and space to check in with the less dominant ones?

We experience internal conflict every time we are not completely present to life. We may be physically present, going through the motions, but our mind is elsewhere, our heart longs for something else and our gut is telling us that we are wasting our time.

Most people dislike conflict. It feels unpleasant. It can escalate and get blown out of proportion. It brings out uncomfortable emotions like anger, resentment, blame and hatred. It disrupts the status quo. It shatters the peace and creates ill will.

Whether it's in your personal life or in professional settings, you will come across people who like to forcefully assert their will in order to be in control. We can't change how others behave, but we can evaluate what makes us tick and how we can respond better. The aim should be to make constructive peace, not to keep an illusion of peace at any cost.

Letting people get their own way for the sake of peace comes at a cost. Conflicts can be averted or resolved when we take time to consider the challenge calmly, take account of the multiple perspectives and have a rational conversation about an agreed way forward.

PART 4

EXERCISES

Try one of the exercises below each day across different situations in your inner and outer world. The examples below for the inner world work just as well in the outer world when there are other people involved.

1. Notice how conflict arises within you. Is your head telling you to do something but your heart is saying something else? Or perhaps your gut is sending warning signs that your heart is choosing to ignore. Simply become aware and, if possible, make a note of these inner conflicts and your usual way of dealing with them.

2. Observe how these inner conflicts are quelled or resolved. Take an inner conflict that occurs repeatedly in your life. For instance, the inner tussle you have every time you see a bar of chocolate that is not in your healthy eating plan. Become an observer of the tussle that occurs within you and how you deal with this particular craving. Who wins and what is the winning strategy? Which amongst your three centres of intelligence most often prevails?

3. This time become a mediator in this conflict. You step in as an external, independent and non-judgemental observer of a particular conflict. Let's say it's around a relationship that you're having difficulty with. Your head, heart and gut have slightly different perspectives on the health

of this relationship and what you should be doing. Take some time to really understand each perspective by following a line of inquiry that begins with what is at the root of this thought, feeling or belief in you? Keep digging until you get to the bottom of the why of that perspective.

4. Get clear on the common goal or desired outcome. What on the surface appears to be the goal is almost never the actual desired outcome. Stay curious by asking questions such as, *"if this, then what?"*

5. Keep the conversation alive. Offer each party the space to verbally ventilate. Make them feel seen, heard and understood. Very often, this paves the way to concessions and compromises.

6. Create clear agreements that cover things like the desired outcomes, the resources needed, who will do what, the time frame you are working with, what happens if something doesn't work, and so on. Agreements are not terms and conditions. The latter come in the spirit of enforcement – do this, or else – and can be a way of limiting one's liability if something goes wrong. Agreements are in the spirit of working together towards a common goal in the spirit of co-operation.

7. Consider what you would do if a conflict cannot be peacefully averted or resolved as above. What is your typical way of dealing with such a situation? How does it make you feel? Is there another way to deal with it that is better for you?

7.

We've explored the meaning of the inner world and the outer world. The inner world is our sense of who we are when we're by ourselves and the outer world is the person we become when we're with others. The core essence of who we are remains the same, but our persona has the potential to take on so many different forms. A bag of flour can be turned into bread or into a delicious cake with icing on top. The flour is the same, but how the world experienced it changed based on how it came together with other ingredients and was reinvented in the process.

Clarity is the freedom from ambiguity. Clarity is knowing who you are, what makes you unique and how you are meant to contribute in this lifetime. In many respects, this is the most important of all the 7C's. It can be both the start and the culmination of our life's journey.

The search for clarity may begin with questions such as:

- Who am I?
- What is my life's purpose?
- Why do I behave the way I do?
- What do I want from life?
- Who do I belong with?
- What are my challenges trying to teach me?

PART 4

RELEASE TO RECEIVE

By now you've done some much-needed assessing and decluttering of your metaphorical backpack. You are feeling lighter and more spacious. The emptiness might feel disconcerting at first. You've just let go of things that have been part of you for so long, and in many ways have become part of your identity. Who are you without them?

It is helpful to remind yourself that you haven't just thrown old forgotten things on a scrap heap. You've acknowledged that these trapped energies, expectations and emotions played a role in your life at one time. They did their job, they helped you survive. You are here because of them. In some cases, in spite of them. They taught you lessons, made you strong and equipped you to be where you are. You thank them and let them go. They can leave you knowing their work is done and that you don't need them anymore.

As you've let go of that which no longer serves you, you've created space and openness to invite the new. This includes ideas, opportunities and people. You might feel freer and lighter than you have in a long time. There is a world of unlimited opportunities and choice out there. This can feel overwhelming if you don't know what you really want or what is right for you.

You need a plan. If nothing else, you need to get clear on what you definitely don't want in your life. The art of selection often begins with rejection. You might find it easier to rule out things you don't want or don't like. Next, you will need to get more intentional and get clear on what you do want and what is right for you.

The expressions Unique Selling Proposition (USP) and brand value are common parlance in the corporate world. These are things that make up the identity of a business and help it stand out amongst its peers. It is the calling card that attracts its ideal customers to the product or service it offers. It is what helps other stakeholders such as employees, suppliers and investors gauge the potential of the business and what it might be worth in the future.

A business has a mission statement, a set of core values and a vision for the future. There will be short, medium and long term goals. These determine the strategy and the actions that need to be taken to create value and turn the vision into reality.

We as individuals can do a similar exercise. I invite you to work through these next steps with someone who can be your personal champion in the form of a friend, partner or coach who can help you see things, especially the good things, about yourself that you're blind to, or are too shy to acknowledge.

Step 1: What makes you unique?

You are unique. For most of your life you might have been rewarded for conforming with the prevailing standards and rules. Now it's time to pause the shapeshifting and get acquainted with the real you. You are invited to create three lists as described below.

List 1: Your Passions

Make a list of things that give you joy and you love doing. They can be big or small, exciting or mundane. They can be things you once did as a child but no longer have the time for, or perhaps have told yourself you are too grown up for. The things you would do for no reason other than because they make you feel happy, peaceful and alive. Some of the things I hear most include being in nature, reading, listening to music, dancing, painting, talking to friends, and so on. Keep adding to the list until you have nothing more to add.

As a separate list under this same main list you could add *a wish list* of things you would love to do someday. Maybe you've always wanted to travel to South America or go bungee jumping or skydive. Write those down. Give those wishes form as a first step to bringing them to life.

List 2: Your Competencies

Note down all the things you do well, things others appreciate about you and those for which you are considered a go-to person. Include skills and traits in your personal and professional life. Perhaps you have a great eye for detail, or your organisational skills have made you the go-to person for arranging family and friendship reunions.

The list can be as long as you want. People often find this exercise difficult because they are so used to thinking about their competencies in the language of their CV or résumé. There can also be a shyness about putting things down that seem mundane. You might think, "Anyone can do that. What's so great about me doing it?" Suspend that kind of judgement. Put every little gift and accomplishment down on that list, especially the ones you know have helped you get things done or help others.

As an adjunct to this list, you can create a wish list of things you'd like to learn or be better at. For instance, you might be quite good at public speaking, but you know you can do better. Maybe you've always wanted to learn Korean so you can travel to Seoul. You loved painting as a child and wish you could learn some of the techniques so you can turn out art that is good enough to be exhibited.

The list of passions and competencies provide a clearer insight into your personality traits and the tools you have within you to make an impact and meaningful contribution to the world.

The third list will acquaint you with your character traits. In a world that is so focused on the visible and the superficial, there is a greater emphasis on the behaviours that make up your personality. If the personality is a car, the person's character is the driver who is less visible to the outside world but is ultimately responsible for getting the car from A to B. Find out how well you really know yourself.

List 3: Your Values

Your values are a consequence of your upbringing, the society you grew up in and the belief systems you hold dear. Some of our values are fairly generic, such as honesty, integrity, loyalty, etc. We might believe they matter and expect it from others. I invite you to go deeper. Discover your core values and non-negotiable beliefs. These will have been formed over the course of your life and will relate more closely to significant life experiences.

Here's what to do:

1. Identify three individuals you admire whom you know or know of. These could be people in your personal life, or in your professional circles, or public figures or celebrities. Make a list of their virtues or traits that elicit your admiration. For instance, if we take the example of Taylor Swift, I admire her single-minded focus, her self-belief, her gift of not taking herself too seriously, and her altruism. The qualities you admire are likely to be character traits you possess within you. Or they could be a role model for the kind of person you want to become.

2. Identify three individuals you know or know of, as above, whom you dislike or disagree with. Make a list of the reasons why you dislike them or disagree with them. Without naming an individual, among the traits I deeply dislike are the woe-me victim mindset and duplicity. The traits on your list will tell you what kind of people you need to stay away from because your values clash with theirs.

3. Another way to identify your core non-negotiable beliefs is to think about a time when you broke off a friendship or meaningful relationship or walked away from a job that you really loved. What were the reasons you made that move? These too will offer clarity on your core values and boundaries.

Step 2: Your Personal Value and Mission Statement

Now that you've got your three lists, take a good look at them and rank them in the order of most important ones at the top. If you have items that are a variation on the same theme – for instance, under passions you may have walking, going on hikes, being in nature and so on. You could put them into one concise bucket titled "being outdoors in nature" or "exercising outdoors".

The Venn diagram below has a circle for each one of your three lists. Each circle will include up to five of the most important items from each list and you will have a snapshot of what makes you unique and how you are creating value in your day-to-day life. When you do this exercise you will most likely find at least one item that appears on all three lists. Something you love doing, that you are also good at and which reflects one of your core values. In this sweet spot lies a clue to what you are meant to be doing.

By focusing positively on the things you love doing, what you are good at and the values that make you authentically who you are, your attention is drawn to the things that you want more of in your life. It highlights your strengths and skills that you know are already making a difference in the workplace and in your personal life.

And lastly, identifying your values will allow you to stay clear of and reject things, ideas, people, places and opportunities that are just not right for you. This level of knowing is a powerful basis for finding purpose, setting goals and creating the life you want. Your values are the ground you

PART 4

walk on. Your vision is the sky above. Your values keep you grounded, especially in uncertain times. Your vision gives you something to aim for and work towards at all times.

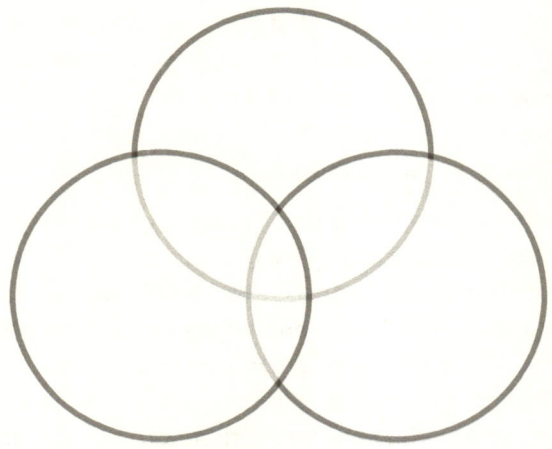

The PCV Venn Diagram

CLIENT STORY: RAHUL DARES TO DREAM

When Rahul came to me he'd turned his back on a promising career in investment banking because it lacked soul. He was also a talented singer and songwriter and had once been a keen cricketer with potential to turn professional.

Now in his mid-thirties and happily married, he dreamed about a job that brought creativity and community together.

One that focused on the human aspect of business, not just making a profit. But money was important too. He wanted music to be a central part of his life's work, but he did not want to be a struggling artist. The challenge was to combine his skills and competencies in areas such as finance with his passion for music and creative thinking.

This is what his three lists looked like:

Passions	Competencies	Values
Music and collaborating with other artists	Making complex things simple	A belief in win-wins, not zero-sum competition
Finding patterns and connecting the dots	Intellectual curiosity and openness	To live and let live
Sports and being outdoors	Good communicator with active listening skills	To be open minded and non-judgmental
Communicating through writing and songs	Good at handling conflict and stay calm in a crisis	That knowledge is power
Giving ideas a fresh vision	Giving structure to other people's ideas and vision	Be in the moment rather than worry about the future

As part of our work together, Rahul understood that what he really wanted was to work for a business whose vision extended beyond making a profit; whose mission was to create wealth for all its stakeholders, not just its shareholders. It now made sense why he had felt so unfulfilled in his previous job in banking.

What once seemed like an impossible dream turned into a happy reality once he had clarity of what he really wanted, what he had to offer that was uniquely aligned with his interests and values, and why this dream mattered so much to him. That awareness helped him spot and create the right opportunities. He was able to clearly and confidently communicate his vision and his values to prospective employers.

He now has a job in which he combines his many valuable skills to help young startups in the creative industries to fulfil their potential. He combines his intellectual curiosity with genuine empathy. He uses his communication skills to create compelling narratives that capture the imagination and tell a story.

Step 3: The vision of your abundant life

Have you ever really wanted something so badly that it was all you could think of? You imagined what it would be like to be in possession of that thing: how it would look, sound, smell, taste and feel. You could picture yourself with that thing so clearly that it was like you were there and it was your reality.

When you get clear on who you are and what you are meant to be doing, it becomes easier to articulate what you really want and the life you want to create. It works on the basis of the frequency of your thoughts and intentions. If you can imagine that there are a number of possibilities for how your life could evolve, you can choose the right one for you by tuning into the frequency of that possibility. And much like a radio station or a TV streaming service, once you've tuned into the right channel, you have the thing you want.

That, in a nutshell, is how you visualise and manifest things. The key to successful manifesting is to see it so clearly as if it was already real and happening to you right now. There's no room for doubt or concerns about any obstacles because as far as your mind is concerned it is your current reality.

The important aspects of creating a clear and compelling vision are:

1. Set your vision for a date that is up to three years from now; it is far enough to create change in your current reality and yet not too far away.
2. Imagine you are already living that life and refer to it in present tense.
3. Include specific details rather than keeping the vision too general or big picture.
4. Believe in it completely, because in your mind this is already a reality.

PART 4

EXERCISE

You're going to take a peek into a vision of your abundant life. You might want to use an audio recorder to help you remember what you see. Find a quiet place where you won't be interrupted. Take a few deep, rhythmic breaths until you feel both relaxed and energised. It's time to wake up your imagination and visualise what your ideal life looks like.

Imagine your life as a house with at least five rooms: a room each for your family, friends, work, me-time and community. In this mind movie you have complete control over the story, the characters in it, the places you go and the things you do.

You are in a time up to three years from now. You are living your abundant life. In this life you have access to everything you need and want. Your future self takes you on a tour of this house, slowly moving from one room to the next. There is no rush. You can linger and experience each room as if you are there, really taking in what you see, hear, feel and sense.

Don't extrapolate from where you are today. Allow the vision of your ideal life to come to you unhindered by your current life and its constraints. As you do this exercise, say out loud what you see and feel. The more detailed your vision the greater clarity you will have on what you need to do to manifest it.

First, you walk in the room called **family**. What does it look like? How does it feel? What do you see? What emotions does it evoke in you? Who else is with you and what do you see yourself doing when in that room?

Next, you move into the room called **work**. What's the setup of this room and what's the first thing you notice about it? How does walking into this room make you feel? What do you see yourself doing? Who else is with you? Colleagues? Clients? How are they interacting with one another and with you? What lights you up when you are in this room?

Next, you move into the room called **friends**. Describe this room and its ambience. Who else is with you? How do they make you feel? How are you spending your time when in this room? How do these friends interact with each other and with you when in this room?

Next, you walk into the room called **me-time**. How is this room different from the other rooms? How do you feel when you are here? How often do you visit this room? Who do you become when you are in this room? What activities do you find yourself pursuing? How much time do you allow yourself to be in this room? How do you feel when you leave this room?

Finally, you walk into the room called the **community**. How does it feel? Who else is there? What do you see yourself and others doing? How often are you able to come here? How does what you do in this room align with the things you care about? How are you making a difference to those in that room with you? Does this room remind you of any of the other rooms in your house?

Your future self who lives in this house is living the balanced, harmonious and fulfilled life you've always dreamed of. This vision is your future. Make it real and specific by adding details to it every time you visit it in your mind's eye.

Give your mind movie colour, texture, sound and even scent. Give it personality. Make it malleable – you can evolve it and let it flow as life does. Every added detail will make it more real and believable.

Beware of doubt creeping in. If faith is health, doubt is disease. Avoid ambiguity. It is no different to placing an online shopping order. Nothing arrives until you have made a clear choice and completed the transaction.

It is not good enough to say that in my ideal life I am successful, happy and wealthy. What does success mean for you? How much money do you need to feel wealthy? How are you defining happiness?

The more clearly you see it, the more powerful and specific your intention will be. The relevant path, people and opportunities will show up for you. Your job is to believe and take the necessary actions to turn your vision into reality.

How visualisation works

Visualisation works because the brain responds to vivid images in the same way that it responds to reality. It is why people who've experienced trauma can feel like they're reliving it when faced with images or thoughts that remind them of it.

Our thoughts and emotions are energy, and they profoundly affect our reality. By changing our thoughts, we can change our reality.

Negative emotions and thoughts can weigh us down and damage our health, as we've already explored at some length. Positive thoughts and mental imagery through clear intention and visualisation can heal us and change our life for the better.

I'd like to share the experience of one client who used visualisation to create the life he wanted and manifested his dream job.

CLIENT STORY - JACK: MANIFESTING HIS DREAM JOB

Right after graduation, Jack landed a role with a PR firm which (at least on paper) was a dream job. But the long working hours and the stressful environment, combined with being constantly judged by his inner critic, wore him down. He quit and went travelling for a year before returning to London. I met him at one of my workshops he'd attended in the hope of gaining some career inspiration.

"It was liberating to have an extended period of time when I didn't have any goals to pursue and was able to take a step back and look at myself and my life afresh. But I needed to return to confront the problems I was running away from."

Jack had returned from his travels with a great deal more self-awareness. He could see how his perfectionism had become a rod for his own back. During his time away he'd learnt to be kinder to himself. He discovered that he finds flow and is happiest when he is being creative, particularly when he is drawing. My workshop was happening at an opportune time for him. He was looking for inspiration on how to create a career out of his love for creativity and art.

Jack and I worked together for six months. In one of our early sessions, I led Jack through a visualisation exercise in which I asked him to imagine he was already living his ideal life. I then asked him to describe what he saw the happier, more fulfilled version of himself doing. At first, Jack found this exercise hard to do, especially when put on the spot during a coaching session. I suggested he try it in his own time, in a tranquil place without putting pressure on himself. In our next session he told me he saw himself earning money from live-scribing and illustrating. He'd be creating works that he would be proud of and would be of value to others. His goal was to work at a global consultancy firm as a facilitator who uses drawing to bring meetings to life and make learning fun.

Our work together involved helping Jack see what made him unique and how he could create value for others and be paid for it. He identified where his strengths lay as well as the areas that needed more attention.

He found role models who inspired him in life and in his chosen line of work. He aspired to be more like them, and they reminded him of his own vision and values. With deepening awareness, Jack grew in clarity and confidence. His goals came into sharper focus, and his efforts towards reaching them took on greater conviction.

Ten months after our first meeting, Jack started his new job at the very same company he'd talked about in his vision. You might say he manifested the job of his dreams. A job that paid him to combine his curiosity and love of learning with the gift of making complex things simple through drawing.

In Jack's case, a few additional personality and character traits, along with some external support, were critical to turning his vision into reality. These include:

- **Conviction** – knowing the what, why and how of his goal

- **Confidence** – a combination of competence and self-belief

- **Commitment** – sticking with it, no matter what

- **Co-operation** – finding people who support you and work with you

- **Courage** – feeling the fear but doing it anyway

What stops us from turning our vision into reality?

When a child is born and has not yet been impacted by the world around it, it is comfortable in its own skin and its pot of self-belief is full to the brim.

As time goes on, even a child in the most nurturing of environments will experience feedback from the ecosystem

PART 4

that will poke holes into this pot of self-belief, causing it to leak. If the pot is refilled with help from nurturing, loving caregivers, then the child will grow up to be self-assured. If such encouragement and support is lacking, the diminishment of self-belief will continue unchecked and the child may grow up lacking confidence and self-worth.

Self-belief and self-worth are the greatest casualties of our hyper competitive and supercritical world. Feedback typically focuses on things we don't do well and how we may overcome our limitations. Even well-meaning parents might be stingy with praise so as not to inject complacency.

What often stops us from achieving our full potential is not our limitations, but rather it is never knowing what we are truly capable of. When we become aware of our strengths and we focus on making the most of them, our limitations become less relevant and easier to overcome.

Maybe you have a dream. Perhaps you've created a vision of a future life in which you are happy, living a life of balance and doing things that give your life meaning. Now you'd like to manifest this life. What might get in your way?

Here are some of the pitfalls to look out for. They all centre on your self-belief, or the lack of it.

1. You don't believe the vision of yourself and your ideal life – it feels too much like a fantasy, a mere product of your imagination.
2. You don't believe you deserve to have that life. Perhaps some old feelings of unworthiness or guilt and shame are lurking just beneath the surface.

3. You don't believe you are ready to take on the risk of going after something that is so fantastic and uncertain. Why leave the mundane certainty of your comfort zone?
4. You don't believe you have it in you to create this life. You're more aware of all your limitations that have in the past blocked your progress.
5. You don't believe you will get the help and support you need to create your dream life.

How to manifest like a boss

How is it that some people are so good at "manifesting" the life they want whilst others stumble at the very first step?

Currently, one of the greatest living examples of manifesting like a boss is megastar singer songwriter Taylor Swift. According to Wikipedia, in 2023, at the age of 34, she became a billionaire with a reported net worth of $1.1bn.

In a 2019 blog post, manifesting coach Caitlin Apple writes about her experience of growing up with Taylor Swift. In it she writes, *"She had this dream... a dream we all thought was a bit odd and far too big. She wanted to be a famous country singer. At nine years old she had this dream.*

"That girl had a dream, a vision, and she never, ever wavered in that dream. She wanted to be a famous singer more than anything else on this planet. Not only that, she truly believed she was going to be, without questioning how or when. She just knew. Yes, she had phenomenal parents (with money) who were overly supportive in backing that dream. But that girl FULLY believed she could. That girl KNEW what she

PART 4

wanted and never stopped trusting that belief. She went after her dream relentlessly, pursuing record companies at eleven years old, and never looked back. She believed in her abilities, her talents, and herself."

Here's what we can learn from Taylor Swift's story.

1. You have to begin with a very clear and specific INTENTION. For Taylor, even as a little girl, her dream was to become a famous country singer. Not just a generic dream of being famous or rich or a singer.

2. You must then put all your ATTENTION behind this intention. No matter what anyone else thinks or says or believes. This is your dream, never mind the doubters. You must not let doubt creep in. The attention needs to be positive and fully aligned with turning your dream into reality. In fact, in your mind, it is already a reality and you are living this dream.

3. Now that you're living it in your mind's eye, it is time to take ACTION to make it real, not just in your mind, but for others too. Note how Taylor worked relentlessly hard pursuing record companies, writing songs from the age of 14 and performing as if she was already a star.

4. Not everyone will "get" you or your dream. There will be detractors, or in modern day parlance, "haters" who don't believe in you and are jealous of your confidence and want to tear you down. What matters is your RESPONSE (not reaction) to such setbacks. Rejection hurts, and you must find ways to process this hurt and disappointment in healthy ways. Putting

some distance and space between the triggering event and yourself is very important. When you are calmer, you remind yourself of your dream that still burns bright, the intention that is as strong as it ever was. You always go back to your intention – it becomes your North Star. You never doubt yourself, even if others doubt you. You never stop believing. And if you are Taylor Swift, you write a hit song about it. More importantly, you sing it with a smile, without a trace of self-pity.

PART 5

PART 5

NO SUCH THING AS AN ORDINARY LIFE

"If you judge a fish by its ability to climb a tree, it will live its whole life believing it is stupid."

ALBERT EINSTEIN

If you measure your life's work by society's skewed standards of greatness, you might live your whole life believing you don't matter.

Have you noticed how society tends to focus on extremes?

You might believe that you can never be interesting (on social media) unless you have a compelling (read jaw-droppingly difficult, amazing or sad) back story. You could be forgiven for thinking that a stable childhood and absence of drama as an adult mean that you are doomed to mediocrity and a life of obscurity.

At one end, society loves the superstars and superheroes. The superstars who are uber talented, beautiful or supremely wealthy, and the superheroes who have overcome extreme adversity and have a back story worthy of Hollywood.

At the other end are those who are either challenging or challenged. The troubled and the makers of trouble. The bad boys and girls who make headlines for all the wrong reasons. Or those who are disadvantaged in some way and need extra attention and resources to improve the quality of their life.

The vast majority of humanity falls into the camp in the middle. People going about their daily life, going to work, paying their taxes and being responsible citizens. Not hogging the limelight nor causing trouble. For that reason, they are likely taken for granted, overlooked or even ignored by society. This pattern of behaviour is evident in families, in classrooms and in workplaces.

If you fall into this camp, you might start to believe that you are ordinary. Nothing special. Overlooked, underestimated and undervalued simply because you are neither a superstar nor a superbrat.

Here's a shout out for being ordinary!

Being ordinary means that you avoid the intrusive scrutiny and limelight that follows those with star qualities. You are not burdened with expectations of people who have an opinion about your life, where you should be going and what you should be doing. You get to quietly create the life you want.

Even "ordinary" people have rich, complex and profoundly interesting lives. But only if you know where to look and ask the right questions. And because every one of us is unique, everyone has the chance of creating an extraordinary life. Back in 2020, I created a podcast titled *Interesting Lives of Ordinary People (iLoOP)*, which shone a light on turning points, transitions and transformations in my guests' lives whose stories were interesting and often inspiring.

MY JOURNEY TO BECOMING THE COACH MY YOUNGER SELF NEEDED

They say a therapist can help you heal your past and live more fully in the present. A coach can help you create your future by helping you see what's possible for you so you can take the right actions.

PART 5

Every coach is different. We each bring our own unique set of experiences and personality traits to the coaching space. Your rapport and relationship with your coach will be one of the most important factors in a successful coaching engagement. The first step is to get clear about what you want from coaching, and then find a coach whose personality, modality and values fits what you are looking for.

The only coach I ever had during my two-decade career in finance was a public speaking coach. He helped me improve my presentation skills, especially when on stage and speaking to a large audience. I had to watch a video of myself and observe my body language, my facial expressions, the pitch and tone of my voice, the cadence and tempo of my speech, etc. At first I found it was intensely uncomfortable having to look at myself and have all my flaws pointed out to me. But it was worth it. I could never have known then just how important public speaking and presenting to an audience would become for me later in life.

I wish I'd taken that experience further and worked with other coaches. Like many people, I was under the impression that coaching was remedial. After all, my employer had paid for me to get public speaking and presentation coaching because they didn't think I was doing it well enough. At least that's what I had told myself. It was only much later that it occurred to me that perhaps they saw I had potential and really wanted me to achieve it more quickly with professional help. A career coach might have helped accelerate my progress by a few years and pointed out to me some of my traits that were not helpful to me. A life coach or therapist might have helped me see more clearly things that were wrong in my marriage so I could have made the necessary changes sooner. I might have made different choices that might have been better for my family and me.

This sort of looking back with regret is helpful only to a point. Aside from making amends and taking the right action – better late than never, professionally, it propelled me to become the sort of coach I would have liked to work with. Someone who was personable and professional. Someone who would really see me, listen to me, hear what I was saying, and help me find my own way.

When I started coaching, I had a ready and willing client. But she was also my most challenging client. She was curious and creative. She was compassionate, particularly towards others. She was courageous but slow to ask for help. She loved a challenge, but often didn't close loops very well. Accountability was a nightmare with her. To date, she's been my most difficult client. This client was, in fact, me.

Somewhere along the way I stopped trying to coach myself. It is far better to pay someone else to do that. I realised that I am a much better coach to clients who are not me! The problem with coaching someone whom you know well is that you are too close to them. You can't be completely objective or non-judgemental. You have preconceptions which colour your idea of who they are and who they can become. If things turn sour, you risk it spilling over into your other relationship with them. It is far better to be coached by someone who treats you with unconditional positive regard without being a friend, colleague or family member.

Coaching myself helped me see that there are so many out there who are like me. Especially like the younger me who needed help but couldn't see it, and later wanted help but didn't know whom to turn to. These are men and women who seem to be so well put together who are craving for clarity on the inside, and freedom on the outside. Talented, hard-working and ambitious individuals who want help to get noticed, validated and elevated in their professional lives.

If you've got this far, I thank you. I hope this book has helped you to see yourself more clearly. To recognise the beauty and wonder of being exactly who you are. To accept that your uniqueness is made up of your gifts as well as your limitations, but that there are no limits other than those you have imposed upon yourself.

CREATE YOUR ABUNDANT LIFE

Picture this. You've been invited by the BIG BOSS about the next steps on your career ladder. You get there with a mixture of excitement and trepidation. The boss has laid out a number of projects that are in a broad range of complexity and difficulty. And you must now choose one.

The fairly straightforward ones will be easier to deal with. The more complex ones will require you to stretch yourself and step outside your comfort zone. And then there will be those that are so challenging that you know they will be a grind from day one.

As in finance, there is a risk-reward dynamic. The reward from successful completion of the project is commensurate with the risk, volatility and difficulty of its execution. The easy ones earn you fewer "rewards" in terms of progression, but the chances of you successfully completing them are greater. The most difficult ones have high rates of failure and you might be back to square one. But, if you are successful, you leapfrog several levels and might even earn a well-deserved sabbatical.

What if we could view our life as an exciting project that we had a role in choosing before we were born? Except that we have no memory of it.

Let's assume we come into this world with our objectives being to learn, to create and evolve until our time is up. There is no rule book. There are no goals, other than to be here in the now. We are meant to figure out our vision and purpose on the job. We will undoubtedly get things wrong. We will feel and inflict pain. We will experience unbelievable joy and love. We will be presented with unlimited choices and chances to grow, to redeem ourselves and to make a difference.

Your body is the vehicle that facilitates your experience of being human. Your senses, your imagination and your intellect are tools that help you make sense of the world and navigate your way through it.

There are three key resources that you must learn to work with and balance if you are to create your abundant life.

1. Energy
2. Time
3. Money

PART 5

Energy

Energy is all around us. It can be neither created nor destroyed, but it flows and changes form all around us and within us. We feel it, we use it, we are it.

Dr David Hawkins was a renowned physician, psychiatrist, spiritual teacher and author of several best-selling books and the creator of the *Map of Consciousness.*

In his book *Letting Go – The Pathway of Surrender* he writes, *"Everything emits energy, either positive or negative. Intuitively, we know the difference between a positive person – friendly, genuine, considerate, and a negative one – greedy, deceitful, hateful. The energy of Mother Teresa was obviously different from the energy of Adolf Hitler. Most people's energy is somewhere between the two. Music, places, books, animals, intentions and all of life emit an energy that can be calibrated as to its essence and its degree of truth. Like goes to like."*

Emotions such as shame, guilt, apathy, grief and fear have very low vibrations. These can keep us in a state of indecision and paralysis. And because like attracts like, a person riddled with these negative emotions will experience events that will make them feel more of the same.

Emotions such as desire, stress, anger and pride have higher vibrations and are likely to propel us out of our misery into taking some action. Courage is where a turning point occurs and it leads unto the more positive emotions that include acceptance, love, joy and peace. Enlightenment is the highest vibration emotion and only a few have ever experienced it.

We can harness our life force by learning to go from emotions that keep us stuck in lower vibrations to those that help us flow in the higher vibrations arena beyond courage. This can be done by first identifying the emotions, acknowledging and accepting their presence and then letting them go. Once we've let go of negative emotions, we allow something else to take its place. At that point, we can choose courage, acceptance, love, joy or even peace.

If the emotion of anger dominates our energy field, we are likely to attract angry people or events that will make us angry. We become tuned into that frequency, like the radio analogy I used earlier, we receive back an experience that is also on that same frequency. Becoming aware of this is the first step.

Let's say you've become aware that you often erupt with anger when you least expect it, and often without justification. You could reflect on this emotion, identify the things that trigger you and go deeper to discover why they make you angry. Curiosity is a great antidote for anything that is unexplained. When you've identified and acknowledged the emotion and gently probed into its root cause, you might find it easier to look at it with a fresh pair of eyes. You might even be able to look at it objectively and find that you no longer feel as angry. There is now potential to move from anger to a more positive emotion.

This is the inside out approach to going from feeling stuck, blocked or depleted to being more energised, motivated and fulfilled. The antidote to depression is creation. Going from feeling depressed to feeling joyful is a really big step, and too big a leap for most to contemplate from the depths of depression. However, to create all we have to do is to get out of our state of apathy and do something. Anything. We have to go into action and creation mode. Once we are moving, we are already climbing up that consciousness ladder into higher states of vibration. Can you now see why some creative people seem so melancholy and often have tragic lives?

Having and upholding boundaries is another very effective way of managing your energy. We can't help being influenced by the energy of other people with whom we interact. Being exposed to disturbing news reports or watching a violent movie impacts our energy. We are impacted by the emotions of those with whom we come into contact. It is natural as we are born with an innate level of empathy. We can become more discerning and mindful in what we expose ourselves to and how we handle the resulting cocktail of emotions.

One of the simplest and most effective ways to regulate and balance our emotions is by making a practice of regularly checking in with yourself. If you find yourself in one of the lower states of vibrations, get curious. Ask yourself what's going on with you. Observe yourself with curiosity and compassion. If possible, label the emotion you are experiencing. By giving the emotion a name, we make it feel seen and acknowledged. Check if you can connect the emotion with an event that might have triggered it. Was the emotion something that you directly experienced, or did you absorb it from someone with whom you came into contact? Once you have an understanding of why you feel the way you do, you will find it is easier to process it, release it and move into a different feeling.

During these check-ins, ask yourself these questions:

- What am I feeling right now?
- What has triggered this feeling?
- Where in my body does this feeling appear?
- What does my body need me to do now?

The answers you get will come from deep within and will be your most trustworthy guide in terms of what self-honouring choices you need to make.

Over time, this process will become a way of life. You will become more aware of the kinds of situations, people and stimuli that make you feel positive. Upholding your boundaries will limit your exposure to things that drain you and make you feel bad. And when you have no control over this, your inner discernment will help you restore balance and harmony from within.

Time

Let's go back to my analogy of the project that became your life that you chose to embark on. You're dimly aware that you have a limited amount of time in which to execute this project, except you don't know how long. All you know is that your mission is to do the best you can with what you have and while you are still able to.

I want you to imagine that when you took life in your mother's womb, you were handed a gift in a sealed container. You had no idea what was in it or how you were meant to use it. You realise later that it is a use-it-or-lose-it gift that can't be replaced, earned nor substituted. And with every passing moment this gift ebbs away and could run out at any time without warning. Crucially, you can't live without it.

If this gift was money, how would you treat it? The gift I am talking about is time. And more specifically the time you have on this earth in your current human lifetime.

In general, people are far more careful with their money than they are with their time. Expressions such as passing the time or killing time suggest there is an abundance of it. Be honest, how often have you chosen to go along to a "free" event without really knowing the value it will add to your life? Would you have made the same decision if you had to pay even a small fee to attend that same event?

Everything changes when you realise that money is abundant and flows freely, whilst your time is a scarce and depleting resource.

We owe it to ourselves to make the most of this precious gift that is our time on this earth. We can become really present and intentional in terms of how we use it. Time, like money, can be spent, saved, invested and given away. Let's look at each in turn.

Spending time is what happens each day anyway and there isn't a lot we can do to stop it. But wouldn't it be great if our time was spent engaged in actions that are meaningful to us and others? Let's say we are waiting for a bus. The bus is running late. We might feel irritated, even agitated by this delay. If we allow this emotion to prevail, we are likely to infect others who are waiting with those negative vibes. Alternatively, we might use that time to look around and observe the beautiful flowers in the garden opposite the bus stop, to smile at the child in the pram waiting for the bus with her mother, or even just spend the time listening to music on our headphones. The timing of the bus is not in our control; however, how we respond to a delay is.

Saving time can be about productivity, whereby you achieve more in the same amount of time. For instance, having a faster broadband service might save on upload and download times. Or it can be about freeing up your time so it can be directed towards something more worthwhile. For example, you might delegate certain administrative tasks to someone else in your team so you can focus your time on winning valuable new business.

Investing time is when you devote your time to an activity, person or place with a view to learning something new or creating value. For instance, you might choose to do some work experience over a month to get a taste of a new industry you're considering a career in. You don't get paid for it, but it teaches you lessons that help you decide if the industry is in fact right for you. Or you decide to take a year off work to do a course that will teach you skills and confer qualifications that make you more attractive in the job market.

Giving time, as the name suggests, is what we do consciously every time we show up for others with no expectation of anything in return. When we visit an elderly relative, volunteer for a good cause or are there for a friend who needs to vent.

Perhaps you lead a very busy life and you might think you have very little control over how you use your time. If this was money we were talking about, would you allow others to control how it was being used? Here are a few questions to help you get an initial measure of how well you are using your time.

Consider an activity, event or experience. Answer the following questions with a yes, no or not sure.

- Did it generate a positive emotion for me (such as excitement, inspiration, love, joy or peace)?
- Did I learn something or teach someone else something new?
- Did it resonate with my core values?
- Did it offer me an opportunity to do something worthwhile, for myself or others?

If the answer to every question is a yes, then you know it was time very well spent.

If you got a smattering of yeses or not-sures, there's work to do. What can you do to make it better?

If the answer to every question was a resounding no, then ask yourself whether next time you can avoid a repeat of this.

If the answer to every question is no, but it is one of those things you can't avoid, then ask yourself what you can do next time to make it more valuable to yourself and others. What could you do that would turn at least one of those noes into a yes?

Remember, you chose this life and your goal is to achieve all you can in the limited time you have. You are going to be evaluated (thankfully not by Yoda) on how hard you tried, the lessons you learnt and the difference you made. It is never too late to create a better life.

Money

There are so many unhelpful myths around money. We may have grown up being told money is the root of all evil, money is scarce, you can't make money unless you work very hard, and so on.

Every one of us has a money story that weaves a complex invisible web that can hold us prisoner and stop us having an abundant mindset.

Money is neither good nor evil. It is a tool that sets us free. And like any tool, it can be put to good use or be an instrument that creates chaos and destruction.

Money isn't scarce. Money is energy, and like all energy it is abundant and free flowing. It does not like being trapped and it won't go where it is not wanted, or where there is resistance.

How is money energy? Money is the currency we use to represent the value we exchange and disseminate in our daily lives. It is the energy of every individual, the collective and the universe that creates this value. Given that this energy is abundant, ergo, so is the potential to create value and hence money.

When there is an economic recession or a financial crisis, it may appear that money has vanished and is harder to access. That is a representation of the energetic field where people are more anxious, fearful and even depressed. They are not creating the value they once were and every contraction has a knock-on impact on those who were previously in an energetic flow of value. We can see why the money flow also contracts as a direct result of this reduced frequency and value creation.

When viewed this way, we can see why some people continue to thrive and make money even in the depth of a great depression. If you can raise your vibration, take the right actions and create value the money will flow towards you.

The relationship between hard work and money is more complex. There is a limited correlation between hard work and money. If working hard meant you made more money, we wouldn't have construction workers, miners, farmers and people in labour intensive jobs living hand to mouth.

Our society and certain religions perpetuate the myths around virtues of pain and hard work leading to beliefs such as no pain, no gain! If you haven't suffered, then you haven't truly earned it. Competing becomes a way of life, where outcomes are seen as a zero-sum game. If I win, then someone else loses. The quantity of the pie is fixed and if I have more of it, I deprive someone else of their share, and vice versa. Obviously, there are areas in our lives where this is so, such as in sport, where if your team wins, then you quite rightly keep the prize and the other teams have to wait until next time to win it back. But this is not true of your life or what is possible for you.

Actions and energetic exchanges from a place of high vibration, i.e. where you are experiencing the emotions in the higher spectrum on Dr Hawkins' logarithmic scale, are more powerful for value creation than actions that are steeped in emotions such as apathy, fear or even anger.

Another important factor in wealth creation is your attitude towards money. Money is drawn to people who value it, appreciate it and create a fertile ground for it to flow and grow. If you believe money is a dirty word, that wealthy people are immoral and greedy, or if you have some other negative mental association with money such as feeling unworthy of it, then it is unlikely that money will flow towards you. Those negative attitudes act like repellants. Your mental blocks create resistance to the free flow of money.

There is an abundance of money floating around. We may have a limited amount of it in our bank account, and that can put constraints on how we spend it. We can attract more money into our lives by creating a product or service that is valued by others enough so they are willing to pay for it. The only things that limit us are our own belief systems and capabilities.

A quick note on the role of the banking system in the abundance of money. If the economy is the human body, money represents the nutrients and oxygen needed to keep it going and the banking system is the cardiovascular system that pumps money across the economy. The central bank is like the heart that pumps harder if the economy needs more money.

The banks need money to flow freely, and the economy needs a strong banking system that can ensure there is an abundant supply of money when and where it is needed. When either of these dynamics becomes impaired, as happened during the financial crisis that began with the Lehman Brothers bankruptcy, it sends shock waves across the system and can bring entire economies to a standstill. Having a thriving and smooth-running banking system that works on trust and trustworthiness is key to a strong economy.

PART 5

As with time, there are broadly five ways in which money flows and creates abundance in our lives.

1. Inflow
2. Expenditure
3. Savings
4. Investment
5. Giving

Inflow of money into your life can be in the form of regular income, passive income or some kind of windfall. When you create an ecosystem that creates value and fosters a positive energy exchange, money is drawn to it. It can be in the form of a salary from regular employment, profits from a business venture, proceeds from the sale of an asset, interest income on savings, or dividends from an investment in shares. Winning the lottery or receiving an inheritance are examples of one-off windfalls.

Expenditure is the outflow of money on goods and services that you may need or want to make your life comfortable. When you spend, you create income for someone else and receive value in return from them. Discernment of price versus value helps us make mindful purchases. What you are willing to pay for a product or service should not exceed its value to you. We create stronger financial foundations when we become more aware of our spending habits and live within our means.

Savings is money in a bank account earning you an interest. As a saver, you are effectively lending money to the bank. Your money is in turn being loaned to an individual or business who is charged an interest that will typically be higher than what the bank pays you. This is the bank's profit. So in a sense, the bank is like a trading company where money is the commodity being traded. Typically, the interest charged and paid is linked to the official interest rate set by the central bank of the country, which in turn is determined by the rate of inflation. High inflation leads to higher interest rates. Consequently, interest rates on savings are a way to provide your money with some protection from inflation whilst keeping your capital safe.

Investment is putting your money into an asset or an endeavour that offers no guarantees, but has the potential, over a longer period of time, to provide superior returns exceeding inflation. So, for instance, you might consider investing in the stock market, which is the most transparent and easily tradable way of investing. Or you might invest in your own or someone else's business because you believe that it will grow its revenues and become more profitable over time. Unlike with savings, and depending on the kind of investment, there is a higher risk of not getting all or any of your money back. But if things go well, you could make a lot more money than if you had simply left it in savings.

Giving is a gift of money as an act of altruism. In its truest sense, you are donating money to a cause or charity without expectation of anything in return. However, in many countries, charitable donations come with certain tax advantages, so in practice even giving comes with benefits. People with genuinely abundant mindsets give when they can in the spirit of letting money flow to where it is needed, believing that it will flow to them in their hour of need. Tithing is an old biblical concept of giving 10% of your earnings. Some of the wealthiest people in the world are also the most consistently philanthropic, which proves that giving makes you richer, not poorer.

PART 5

CREATING A STRONG FINANCIAL FOUNDATION

People often spend a disproportionate amount of time and energy towards generating higher levels of income. They don't pay enough attention to how the money they already have is being used.

Don't just work hard for your money, make your money work harder for you. If you want to build a bright financial future, you must first lay down a strong foundation that takes into account the above five ways in which money can flow.

A strong foundation has four well balanced pillars:

- **Protection** – these are provisions you make to protect yourself and your family in the face of unforeseen and destabilising events affecting your health, belongings, income or life. A combination of relevant insurance and a pot of "rainy day savings" or an emergency fund can act like a safety net, especially in places where there isn't a social or family support system.

- **Savings** – in addition to saving for emergencies, you may have some short term (less than five years) goals, such as buying a car, going on a dream holiday or even saving for a deposit on a house. Putting money aside into easy access or fixed savings accounts is a disciplined and low risk way of working towards such goals.

- **Investments** – for goals that are longer term (over five years) that are less immediate but certain nevertheless – such as getting married, starting a family or saving for your young children's higher education. Investing on a regular basis is a great way to let your money grow and really work for you over time.

- **Pensions** – when you are young, retirement can seem so far away into the future and hence not important. But with increasing life expectancy, people are surviving for two or three decades after they've retired. Any health complications can make retirement more expensive than we could have imagined. The sooner we can start to put money into a pension pot, the longer it has to grow and the effects of compounding over time can be exponential.

DISCERNMENT OF VALUE

As an investor, I would often hear the saying, it is better to travel than to arrive. In stock market parlance, this meant that the share price was already factoring in any good or bad news even before the news was actually confirmed. And so it is in life. The mistake we often make is to focus so completely on the destination that we forget to enjoy the journey.

Your life is not a competition. It is your unique opportunity to create an experience that means something for you. The rewards are in the form of the memories you made, the relationships you shared, the knowledge you learnt and the legacy you leave behind. You get to decide what is most important for you and how you get there.

We've explored the three key elements to creating and measuring abundance – Time, Energy and Money. Every one of us has our own recipe for abundance using those three ingredients. For some, having unfettered time to be in nature, to spend it on activities that give them joy and to be with the people they care about is most important. For others, abundance might mean the ability to have material wealth to elevate their own lifestyle, invest in ideas, things and people that will generate further wealth and wellbeing.

Often it is hard to measure the value created by the things we do or know or experience. Money is the standard currency for measuring value and it works best for things that are standardised with a "market" with clear supply and demand dynamic. What about things that are not standardised? What about things that may have value only to us and are not easily measured or tangible?

You can discern the value in terms of time, money and energy. When you consider a product or service, ask yourself these questions:

1. Did it save time?
2. Did it free up time so it could be directed towards something more worthwhile?
3. Did it save money?
4. Did it help attract new money?
5. Did it create positive intangible outcomes such as joy, learning, good health, peace of mind, security, etc.

When you are living your abundant life, creating and recognising value in this way will become second nature. It doesn't mean you will never fail or make mistakes. It means that when you do, you will see it for what it is and learn from it. The value will lie in the lesson and the wisdom it will bring.

CONCLUSION

If you're like Harry in the film *When Harry Met Sally*, you might be starting at the end to help you decide whether to read the whole book. In which case, I hope this section offers a summary that piques your curiosity about the rest of the book.

If you're a more traditional reader who follows a linear path from start to finish, I thank you for trusting me and well done for staying the course. To really benefit from the book, the ideas and concepts in it must be experienced and experimented with.

The first reading is your opportunity to notice which bits resonate with you and why. The next time you read it you might view those same things in a slightly different light and find new things that you hadn't noticed before.

You must allow these new insights to percolate through your conscious mind into your heart where you feel its impact on your life, and finally to become embedded into your subconscious mind as a new way of being. This takes time and consistent application. You've taken the first important step. Now follow your curiosity and allow yourself to go with the flow.

PART 5

Creating your abundant life is a fine balance between the *what-ifs* that represent possibility, and the *what-is* that is about being truly present to life. This book and my work is about helping you find your flow so you seamlessly combine the state of presence with the openness to what is possible for you.

An abundant life awaits you, no matter who you are or what your past or current circumstances might be, there is always another way, another choice, another life you can create. It begins with believing in your ability to change your reality and use your imagination to paint a picture of what is possible for you. What is a mere possibility today is a reality in a different version of your life. Learn to energetically tune into the frequency of that version of reality.

In this book we cantered through a framework that begins with the metaphorical backpack and how its contents affect your health and personality. We delved into why people stay stuck and unhappy without knowing why they feel that way. Becoming aware that you feel this way and that there is another way is the first step to making a change.

We examined the concept of an abundant life and what you can do to get clear on what that means for you. What does it take to create a life in which you are thriving, not just surviving? I shared stories of Tara, Sam and Alka who have faced this challenge and realised it is not how they want to live.

We talked about how you create your future. You must first establish what you have, what you need to let go and what must be given the space to come into your life. Anamika's story was a reminder that we must release to receive. By letting go of old habits and trapped emotions that no longer serve us, we can create space for new experiences. We can learn more positive ways to respond to triggering stimuli and accept fresh opportunities for growth.

We explored the difference between our inner world and the outer world, and how self-awareness is about how we see ourselves and how we show up in the world. Divya's, Madhu's and Vidya's experiences and emotional responses beautifully illustrate the role our upbringing plays in the shaping of our personality. Connecting the dots of our childhood experiences can often open our eyes to why we behave in certain ways.

Darshana's story is a powerful reminder of the role others play in holding up a mirror to us. Seeing ourselves through the eyes of others can be very powerful, since most of us are not very good at seeing ourselves as others see us. Rajul's experience reminds us that even however clear and confident we might be, there are many things over which we have no control. Letting go of illusions of control can set us free to go towards other possibilities that are often better than we might have considered.

We scrutinised the role of the persona and how it helps us fit into a fickle world that may not respect or value our authenticity. Having and upholding our boundaries and learning discernment in a changing world will help us navigate life with greater self-belief and self-compassion.

I introduced you to my 7C's framework as a guide to becoming more aware of who you are, why you are the way you are and how you can create your abundant life.

1. Curiosity is the art of asking questions and being open to all possibilities. Tulika offered a refreshing

glimpse into a life led from a place of curiosity and conscious change. I then invited you to turn a curious gaze towards yourself and see yourself as if for the very first time. It is an important step towards becoming present and observing yourself without judging or wanting a specific answer. We begin life as intensely curious children. Staying curious can open doors to a life beyond the realm of what we previously considered possible.

2. Creativity is the ability to create something that did not previously exist, with the help of curiosity, imagination and resourcefulness. We talked about the mistaken belief that creativity is something only right-brained people have, and we explored ways we can be more creative in our day to day lives. I shared the story of Priya, the scientist whose life was turned upside down when her brain tumour returned after 11 years in remission. Unable to do the job she once loved, or to even frame her thoughts into words due to Aphasia, she found joy and solace as she communicated through her paintings.

3. Competence is the ability to do something capably and to its conclusion. In today's world, the word is linked with competition, qualifications and recognition. We met Aadhya to whom it really mattered that she had what it takes to be respected as a leader. She talked about her daily self-improvement routine that was driven by how others had responded to her. When we get curious and creative, competence can become intentional and aligned with our interests and life's purpose.

Understanding our own unique learning styles can accelerate and deepen how and what we learn.

4. Connection is ubiquitous but we are often unaware of it. The whole universe is connected in an infinitely intricate and highly sensitive web. Invisible energetic bonds connect us from within and with the outside world. The body remembers everything and keeps track of every experience, sensation and emotion. Becoming more aware and creating more conscious connections can really help us navigate our way through life with greater equanimity and balance. For Nivedita, yoga and connecting with her breath helped her slow down, take greater notice of the world around her and what was going on inside her. Nehaarikaa learnt the importance of creating strong connections, both with herself and others, and the little rituals that matter in relationships.

5. Communication occurs as an energetic exchange of messages that is constantly happening, but we are consciously aware of only a fraction of this. The different parts of our body are communicating with each other and getting on with the task of keeping us alive. We explored verbal, non-verbal and interspecies communication. Rose shows us how simple it is to connect more deeply with our bodies by listening to it, journaling the things we notice. It helps her connect the dots and build a deeper understanding of what's going on in her inner world. Communicating with others too is much more effective when we learn to listen more attentively and observe the non-verbal cues that are often more reliable narrators.

6. Conflict is an inevitable consequence of living in a world where there are as many opinions, desires and outcomes as there are people. Understanding the role conflict plays in creating change and growth can help us spot it, avert it and resolve it in positive ways. I offered my own example of conflict avoidance and the price we pay when we keep the peace at any cost. Dhanashree avoids conflict with people she doesn't know well or doesn't trust by limiting her interactions with them. Darshana has perfected the art of handling disagreements with people she knows well by getting clear on what she wants to say and waiting for the right time to have a potentially difficult conversation.

7. Clarity is the result of deeper awareness and acceptance of what's going on within us, who we are, how we interact with the outside world and what we really want in life. We can remember what gives us joy, what we're good at doing and what our core non-negotiable beliefs and values are. Understanding ourselves better in this way can help us get clearer on our life's purpose and mission. This creates a good basis upon which to visualise what an abundant life looks like for us and how to manifest it like a boss.

I hope that this book has given you food for thought. Let it be a reminder that wherever you are in your life today, you matter and your work is not yet done. Unseen forces are here to support you and spur you on. Take a look at yourself and the world you live in with a fresh pair of eyes, with a new sense of wonder and purpose.

You may already be living a great life. Perhaps you just never paid attention to it because you were too busy comparing yourself to someone else. Gratitude is a powerful fertiliser that helps nourish that which is already good in your life and attracts more reasons to be grateful. But even with gratitude for what you already have, you can strive for more, for something different.

Your abundant life awaits you. Not as some far away destination in the future, but right here in your mind's eye, on a frequency that is a mental flick of a button away. Tune into it and enjoy the ride.

ACKNOWLEDGEMENTS

So many people helped me bring this book to fruition, not always knowingly. I am grateful to you all.

Thank you to my book coach and editing team at Known Publishing. Ben Watkins, is the kindest, sweetest and most patient of people without whose encouragement this book would never have seen the light of day. He helped me create a lucid structure within which my words could flow. Henry Harding, along with his design and editing team, gave the words form so that they leapt off the pages making them an easier and more enjoyable read.

I am so proud of my son Yuvi, who created the illustrations for this book, adding a child-like innocence that resonates beautifully with the messages in it. Thank you to my dear friend Asha Mandapatty for reading the early draft of my manuscript and for suggesting I add illustrations. Thank you to my friend and former colleague Jennifer Ramsey for taking time out of her busy schedule and giving me invaluable feedback. Your thoughtful observations and suggestions helped me to rethink and rewrite some of the key aspects of this book.

A huge thank you to all those who shared their stories and perspectives with me for this book. You know who you are. I am so grateful to my clients who are my inspiration and my teachers. Every person I have ever interacted with has helped me see my world through their eyes and the prism of their experiences.

Thank you to my friends and extended family whose kind words have been a source of great encouragement in all my creative pursuits. I am grateful to children who keep me grounded and are there for me when I need them. But most of all, I want to say thank you to the child in me who still waits patiently for the day when she is free to experience joy and laughter without a care in the world.

ABOUT THE AUTHOR

Rohini grew up in India into a family that was a blend of progressive and old-fashioned conservatism. At the age of 23, freshly graduated from IIM-Bangalore, one of India's top business schools, she arrived in the UK on a diplomatic passport to experience a different way of life for a limited time. She calls herself an accidental immigrant and now, three decades later, calls England her home.

The early years after moving to London were enduring lessons in humility and resourcefulness. Looking back, it is clear that those were the most valuable of life lessons that no formal education could have ever provided. Rohini got her first real career break six years after arriving in the UK when she got hired by a London-based wealth management firm where she worked for 18 years. She flourished in a culture of intellectual curiosity, openness and innovation. In 2015 she took early retirement from a corporate career.

In 2016, Rohini published her first book *Leading Ladies* which paved the way towards becoming a life coach. Over the years she has followed her curiosity and been led by her clients' needs adding different modalities to her coaching toolbox. She is a certified deep transformational coach, an ICF accredited coach (ACC), a certified emotion code practitioner, a personal finance coach and a practitioner of the enneagram personality type system.

Rohini has helped clients create personal and professional breakthroughs. She has helped hundreds of individuals view themselves with fresh pairs of eyes and explore what's truly possible for them. She combines nearly three decades of business, finance and life experience with her ability to make her clients feel seen, heard and understood.

Rohini is the author of *Leading Ladies: inspiring stories of women who found their purpose with passion*. She is the host of the podcast *Interesting Lives of Ordinary People*. She finds joy in nature, walking, hula-hooping and music.

You can get in touch with her and find out more about her via:

www.rohini-rathour.co.uk

www.youtube.com/channel/ UClsUVzuWaHfxmQonsDEauKQ

www.linkedin.com/in/rohini-rathour

info@rohini-rathour.co.uk

www.ingramcontent.com/pod-product-compliance
Lightning Source LLC
Chambersburg PA
CBHW030256100526
44590CB00012B/420